"I have had the pleasure of walking alo
I have never known a more tender-hearted yet fiercely powerful wo
words are raw, beautiful, and speak to the power within us all to rise up and begin again."

—**MEREDITH DUNN**, *founder and CEO, Freedom Press*

"Wow! I couldn't stop reading! Honestly, it had me gripped from start to finish. The Dear John letter is so powerful. Your emotions are raw but not too much. I think it's honest, real, and true.

It is what other people in bad situations need to hear, so they too can be woke! I can't wait to read the whole book!"

—**JOANNA WICKHAM**, *creative writer*

"I have had the honor of watching Seme as she wrote *When the Fog Lifts*. She is a go-getter and smart and has poured herself into the birth of this book. Seme's courage and fight is captured on every page. Seme's words are encouraging and straightforward and show us we can overcome and start over again."

—**STACEY ROBINSON**, *owner and CEO, Regal Elegance Boutique*

"I've known Seme for a couple of years now. As her friend and professional colleague, I've found her to be strong, kind, and intelligent. What I admire the most is her ability to be candid in high-stake situations and her willingness to adapt to new ideas."

—**LANRE ELDEE DABIRI**, *IT consultant and real estate investor*

"Wow! A racy, yet intimate account of a young girl in a foreign land, struggling through college, and finally ending up in a relationship that in the end was toxic. Her overly protective childhood did not prepare her for the realities of life. Now caught between an emotionally abusive husband and childhood memories of a very different situation with her parents, Seme gives a brutally frank account of her experiences. One can see how she struggles through the years. The initial hope that things will get better, the gradual and painful realization that the converse is the case, the initial period of denial, and, finally, after three children and one and a half decades later, the sad realization that this was a lost cause. Apart from telling a tale that is really riveting and holds the reader spellbound, the real reason for writing the book is to encourage other glassy-eyed ladies to look deeper before getting into serious relationships. This noble objective, in which the author bares her heart to the reader, makes this book at once so readable and a must-read for for young ladies."

—**DADDY! FESTUS UNUIGBE**, *CEO, Innotech Nig. Ltd.*

"Seme has put herself out there while writing this book, and this only confirms what I already know of her as a selfless, sacrificing sister, mother, wife, and friend. Many conversations on adulting need to be had, and she asks all the right questions."

—**DOLLY LATINWO-BELO**, *Chapman Hall Premier Realtors*

"The writing style of this first-time author screams *New York Times* Best Seller. A definite pick for Oprah's Book Club. What an amazing story of vulnerability, transparency, strength, and accountability.

Her gift to connect draws you in and makes you feel as if you were walking hand in hand with her as she navigates through this journey called life. As a daughter, sister, wife, and mother, Seme relates and closely resembles our own journey in more ways than one. For those who haven't already gone through a similar situation, this book is a handbook, guide, sort-of blueprint on how to navigate or outright avoid dramatic and traumatic situations by giving us an opportunity to take frequent pauses to just reflect before it affects the rest of your life.

As she's figuring out who she is, she somehow manages to encourage the reader to find out who they are. I am almost certain that *When the Fog Lifts* was her way to begin self-healing, but what she has also managed to do is help other women like me do the exact same. This is a must-read!"

—**AASIYA MUSLIM**, *CEO, Portpholiio*

"*When the Fog Lifts* is the beautiful story of a woman learning to find herself in the midst of hardship and pain.

Seme's tender recollections of growing up in a home filled with love and happiness gave her hope and a road map for the family she wanted to have one day. But like many women, she found herself married to an unsupportive spouse and learned very quickly how to be the provider, the disciplinarian, the educator, the nurturer, and the decision maker.

In her book, Seme shares her raw emotions and vulnerability as she questions her reality. She goes on to tell her brave account of stepping away from a marriage that she tried so hard to preserve and learning to put her faith and trust in her Heavenly Father to guide her along the way."

—**RUTH UNGERER**, *personal wellness coach, BodybyRuth.com*

"*When the Fog Lifts* is a powerful and insightful journey of a precious, beautiful soul who has been shaken up, but who is also ready to move into a bright future. Seme's raw and honest style of writing really draws you in and takes you on her journey with her—not to mention, it's just a blessing to know her!"

—**CHARISSA NEWELL**, *co-founder and art director, twolineSTUDIO*

DISCLAIMER

Although the publisher and the author have made every effort to ensure that the information in this book was true and correct at the time of publication, and while this publication is designed to provide accurate information in regard to the subject matter covered, the publisher and the author assume no responsibility for errors, inaccuracies, omissions, or any other inconsistencies herein and hereby disclaim any liability to any party for any loss, damage, or disruption caused by errors or omissions, whether such errors or omissions result from negligence, accident, or any other cause.

Some names and identifying details have been changed or omitted to protect the privacy of individuals.

This publication is meant as a source of valuable information for the reader, however it is not intended as a substitute for the medical advice of physicians. The reader should regularly consult a physician in matters relating to his/her health that may require diagnosis or medical attention. Neither the author nor publisher of this book are, nor do they purport to be, licensed medical professionals. Any references to the human psychological state, or any other medical condition or diagnosis, as well as any advice contained herein is based completely upon the author's opinion and firsthand experiences only.

SEME EROH

WHEN THE FOG Lifts

GAINING CLARITY AFTER CHAOS & CONFUSION

- A COLLECTION OF ESSAYS -

SEMERITY CONNECTIONS

www.SemeEroh.com

ATLANTA, GEORGIA

When the Fog Lifts
Gaining Clarity After Chaos & Confusion – A Collection of Essays

Semerity Connections

www.SemeEroh.com

ISBN 978-0-578-77705-4

Written by Seme Eroh

Cover and interior designed by Charissa Newell – www.twolinestudio.com © 2020 All rights reserved – used with permission.

TABLE OF CONTENTS

DEDICATION

To my Almighty Father for love, strength, grace, mercy, and conviction.

To my parents for always loving and supporting me.

To my children for not breaking through it all. I love you, Nathan, Stephanie, and Danielle.
I hope this book helps light your path in life.

To my extended family and friends for believing in me and knowing me enough to trust my decisions.

To my readers, I shared this story for you to take a page or pages from this book and learn from my mistakes and strength.

Thank you.

PREFACE

Writing has always been therapeutic to me. I've always known I wanted to write a book, but I didn't know about what. I knew I had a story to tell, but I wasn't sure if it was okay to share so much about myself and how people would receive it. So I journaled. And then I stopped because I had no privacy. Then I started again, trying to make my writing illegible so no one could read it—not even me.

I'm a forty-two-year-old woman from Edo State in Nigeria. I grew up in Lagos, Nigeria with my parents and my brother and sister. We were upper-middle-class when I was younger. When I was about eleven, my dad left paid employment and started his own company. We became the family of an entrepreneur.

My mom was a seamstress. We moved from company-provided housing in the city to the suburbs, or the "boonies," of Lagos. That was when I started to see that things were changing, but my parents made sure they maintained a certain level of our old life. In the first few years, my dad's business flourished, and then after a couple more years, he started to realize that he was indeed a scientist and not a businessman. He also was not cut out for the business landscape of Nigeria. He was not ready to sacrifice his integrity to get ahead. So we lived the saying, "Your reward is in heaven life."

We managed. We all graduated from the best elementary schools in Lagos: Corona Schools Apapa and Gbagada. I'm sure it was tough for my dad, but he made it work. By the time I was in high school, things were different, but we managed and were a very close and loving family. My mom still did not work—my dad still assumed the responsibility of taking care of the expenses in the home. It wasn't even a conversation. I grew up seeing my dad doing what it took to provide for us. Oftentimes, that meant late deliveries of big envelopes of money to my already-agitated mother. No matter what, my dad came through.

The stress, however, took its toll. He became hypertensive. My mom slowly started to do her part, but the roles were never misunderstood. The role of the provider was always my dad's. That was their agreement. But they also were a team, and they picked up the slack for each other. It is for those times when you cannot do it, like my dad, that you save up your support credits. (This is like the analogy that you pay into the bank with the hope of withdrawing one day. My dad had paid in for years, and he was now withdrawing. My mom remembered and had no hesitation to step up.) I saw this with my parents. My mom knew that if and when my dad could, he'd show up.

It was with this upbringing that I came to the United States of America, bright-eyed and bushy-tailed. Naive as all get out. I came to go to college, and again my dad paid my fees and supported me for most of my time in undergrad. I wanted to be a corporate lawyer, and then I changed majors to computer information systems because it sounded cool, and I didn't want to take a million bar exams because my plan was always to go back home to Nigeria after getting my master's degree. I didn't know that I would fall in love and decide to stay in the U.S. No regrets!

I dated and lived my life, but I never realized how important our upbringing is in shaping our lives. I know we say it, but I didn't get it until I was thirty-seven years old. I remembered my friends' parents and their interactions. I remembered my parents. And now I observed my friends back home and here in the United States and how they dated and spent their money, how they lived their lives, their values, and their attitudes. And I started to see what the old wives meant by upbringing and how it affects us.

I was easygoing, not a fighter, very trusting, and a people pleaser. It was uncomfortable for me to ask for money. I was very independent, scared to assert myself and take what's mine. And part of me was broken. The part that was broken didn't attract the right type of partner.

I dated my ex-husband for three years, and in that time we lived together. I gave into a lot of things that I should have had boundaries or been stronger about. I ignored a lot of things I should have not ignored. I did not fight or recognize problems when I should have stood my ground. I shared my weaknesses and deep secrets too early. I made myself vulnerable. Most importantly, I did not know myself before adding another human to my equation. It didn't add up.

My forty-second birthday is on Monday, August 24, 2020, during this unfortunate COVID-19 pandemic. I am almost divorced with three children. I have way too much responsibility. This is not at all where I imagined myself to be at this time in my life, but it is what it is. I tried very hard to keep my family together at great financial, emotional, spiritual, and physical cost to myself. Family is very important to me, and I will never give up on family. I am sharing my story with you with the hope that it resonates, with the hope that it causes you to reflect, see your worth, and leave destructive habits and relationships behind and helps you course correct.

I have made many mistakes and have had many, many blessings. But I have also seen a lot, and I want to share this with you. I am what some call an "empath." Some may ask throughout this book, like my friends have asked me, "Why didn't you fight?" "Why didn't you speak up?" I did as much as I could with what I knew how to do at the time. I also lost myself on this journey, but I am finding myself again and healing. Writing this book is a key tool in my healing journey. This book is about a girl who went through life blind. Blind as a young girl, blind as an immigrant, blind as a girlfriend, blind as a woman, blind as a mother, and blind as a partner or wife.

Please hear my heart in these words. I found myself in a situation that just didn't go as planned. I have tried to be as candid as I can, but with being candid comes the uprooting of some feelings that I am honestly still resolving on my own. So, some may feel I have said too much, but I cannot share a half story. I have also had many say to me, "You shouldn't write a book while you're still hurting." I appreciate the feedback, but I also do not want to write to you three to five years from now, when I am brand new. How will you know that process? How will you grow? How will I help you with my perfect story, all tied up nicely with a bow? How will you know how I achieved my peace? I would have forgotten, and I don't want to forget.

So, let me write to you now, when it is fresh. My friends who advised me to wait mean well, but I am different. I will send my message and try not to write bitterly, but I cannot please everyone. Learn what you will. I have to present this story from my viewpoint and hope that it does not come off as me being negative or bitter. I am not bitter, just hurt—but I am also not staying in my place of hurt. I am moving on with my life, and I honestly see more clearly now. I feel my peace growing more and more. I no longer depend on others for my happiness or peace. I look above to the Lord, and He has blessed me with three beautiful gifts in my children.

My children, please understand that the stories I share are not meant to cause you pain but to prepare you for life outside of our home and how cruel the world can be. It is not to shed a bad light on anyone, but to make you aware that life must be lived intentionally and that when choosing acquaintances, friends, and even partners, you do have the right to be picky and stick to your values, which I hope I have instilled in you. Please know that I am your mother and I love you dearly, but it is my job to let you know where I made mistakes and may have misled you in what life looks like. This book is my vehicle to do that.

My hope for this book is to help everyone see different perspectives and to see how your experiences and viewpoints influence how you live your life. I also hope that it gives you the courage to stop living in brokenness, decide to choose another path, and heal.

I don't claim to have the answers. I just want to share my personal experience and the conversations I have had with several people—both men and women—to help provide a different point of view.

"Don't apologize for opening your eyes."

—SE

Part 1

"Even if you're a fly on the wall,
you are still affected by what
happens around you."

ME AND MY MARRIAGE

My main reason for my writing this book, apart from what I have explained in the preface, is understanding and appreciating human complexity. In my journey to share my experiences and perspectives through writing, I have had the opportunity to gain a deeper insight into myself and discover more about myself. One of the things I found out through working with my coach is which characteristics I fear most. These are negativity, deceit, manipulation, and complexity.

The most active one of those fears is complexity. It keeps me in a state of confusion and guessing. I always feel like I'm in limbo, unstable.

When dealing with complex people, I want to understand them more (especially in a close relationship like marriage), and it drains me because my mind is not complex. I am very uncomplicated. What you see is what you get. Remember, I am an empath.* We tend to take on other people's complexities and problems, which drains us. That is not to say I am simple—I just feel things very deeply and absorb things in many layers. See…not so simple!

My husband was a very complicated person. I was always in a state of limbo with him because I never knew where I stood. What had I said or done wrong? I was always questioning myself and wondering when the other shoe would drop. He would suddenly be upset with me for no reason or return from a day out with a scowl, and my heart would be in my throat. I would be scared of what had happened this time. I

***See Glossary on page 270 for definition.*

never got an explanation of what the real issue was. Perhaps there was no real issue. All I got was the run-around until I felt like I had done something wrong.

I lived in a state of fear—of never knowing what was going on inside his mind and with his emotions. I never felt as though I got to the heart of his thoughts. He kept them locked away. Out of reach. This emotional withholding created doubt, questioning, insecurity. It was an awful way to live, and it's one of the main ways he asserted his control over me.

I started to observe this dynamic with other relationships and hear it in conversations with friends and clients. They would express that they would give anything to know what was going on in their partner's mind. Some would say that in the few instances when their partners told them what they were really feeling, it was a far cry from what they thought. It would always be so trivial and incoherent. That's why they made you guess...because it wasn't worth saying out loud.

What roles do our partners really see themselves playing in our lives? This is a very good question, and if you hear some of the offhand comments I have gotten around this, you will reel with shock. Some have the traditional beliefs that a woman takes care of the home literally in every sense. But what happens when the woman also works full-time? Some think that as long as they provide financially, they don't need to provide any other type of support. Some refer to their children as their wife's children. Some only want to be involved in activities that can be noticed by others. These are just a few examples.

Many people in marriages feel as if they are "helping their partners" or doing them a favor with things that concern the whole family. Women often leave all the financial responsibility to their husbands, and men leave all the household duties to their wives. Is this fair?

I am thinking these guys are thinking, "I pay all the bills. She can do the rest of it." And the women are probably thinking, "He goes to work all day and leaves me with these kids. He better pay all the bills!"

Where's the balance? What about my situation, where I did both? I was the default; my husband "helped me" from time to time. There's that word again. Can you really "help" with your own kids? Some say he was going to keep withholding or punishing me because he felt he has done his part. Is there really a line where your responsibility in your home, to your spouse and children, stops? Should there be? My ex-husband would say to me, "You want division of labor, right? Okay. I'll give it to you." He was right. The way I presented, it was like I wanted division of labor. But what I really wanted was a plan and an agreement, or just for us to have each other's backs. What would have been enough for him in this case?

I still don't know, but if given the opportunity, I would have asked him:

What are you thinking?

What's the plan?

What's the result here?

You vowed to love and honor me. Do you not see me suffering, stressed, and in pain? Do you just not care? Isn't love supposed to give and sacrifice? Are you lying, or have you just gotten comfortable? Don't you see me hustling? Don't you care that I had a bad day at work or that I'm just tired? Or maybe I'm not tired…can you just tell me to take the day, go to the spa? "I'll pay you for today, so you can really rest, go shopping, go and take a nap." Or even better: "Let me take some of this off you permanently. It's what I should be doing, anyway."

I don't know, dang! Something! Why is it so difficult for you to see me as a woman, a partner, someone's daughter, and just a human being? I sure don't want to wear the pants, but sometimes I forget because I kind of live a role reversal, but it's not reversed. It's a role inheritance. I do my role and yours full-time, and you do yours less than part-time. You don't even see it as a job because you don't show up every day. I show up even if I don't want to. If I were your boss, I would have fired you. Well, I guess I did! Boom!

I'd ask, What the heck are you thinking? And when is this going to end? We are going on sixteen years of this situation. Are you ever going to get it together, or am I going to have to keep tiptoeing? Tell me what the flip you're thinking because I want to know, darn it!

Are you unwilling? Or are you unable?

I found that I have had different answers to these questions about my ex throughout my time writing this book, but I had confirmation in the end. I no longer need to keep asking the question.

Perspective

No, you cannot read minds, and you should not be expected to. As of today, I still don't know what the flip he was thinking, but it cost us our family and marriage.

I made my peace about two years ago by not trying to figure out what he was thinking or feeding into the mood swings. I had my hands full. Maybe he didn't even know what he was thinking or what effect it had on me. He was quite self-absorbed. Who knows?

If it is worth hearing, you will hear about it. Just do your best and be supportive without hurting yourself. Long-term second guessing and whatever it is I went through are detrimental to your physical and mental health. My therapist said I was a victim of some traits of narcissistic personality disorder in the form of mental manipulation. I still don't identify as a victim of anything, which I'll talk about later in this book.

I don't believe my husband was intentionally hurting me or not seeing me, but he had been doing those things for years without any repercussion. It does not make him a bad person, but it makes him negligent of his role in my life and our marriage. It shines a light on the fact that he is also deeply wounded and was acting out of his own pain and suffering. I just happened to be the recipient of it all. SMH. What a conundrum!

I cannot tell you what your specific situation is like or going to be like, but you cannot wait for someone to truly see and understand you and your needs. You must see yourself and take care of yourself.

You cannot read minds. Being a fly on a wall is just a figure of speech—not possible. Even if you're a fly on the wall, you are still affected by what happens around you. Guard your heart, live your life, and work on yourself. Do what makes you happy.

Proverbs 4:23 says:
"Guard your heart above all else, for everything you do flows from it."

Discussion & Reflection Questions:

- How do you communicate with non-communicative people?
- Have you always been assertive, or do you find it hard to assert yourself?
- Do you believe in roles in marriage/relationships, or do you think people should just feel each other out?

Use the following journal pages to write out your thoughts.

THE LETTER

I will never forget the smell of the letter. How cool it felt in the hot African summer.

It felt and smelled like life itself. It was filled with hope and promise. It reset my dreams and gave me more to focus on.

I lay on the couch in my parents' home in the summer dusk. No electricity—the power transformer was broken for the hundredth time. They would fix it, but it always took an act of God. I spent my days after graduating from high school daydreaming and reading romance novels. I was, and think I still am, a romantic. The highlight of my day was walking to my best friend's house or to my best cousin's house, and then escorting each other back home. We usually stayed in someone's house during the hot afternoon and started our walking in the evening.

The neighboring house would be burning the brush from the day's gardening. You could smell the smoke. You could see parents arriving from work and the faint sound of their families welcoming them. We would talk about our dreams and wait for my dad to return from work so we could put on the generator for power and air conditioning. My dream was to become a lawyer like my aunt, whom I admired so much. I'd work as a corporate lawyer. Maybe one day, I'd become a company secretary. I assumed family would fall in there somewhere.

My mom had gone to the U.K. for medical treatment and surgery, as our medical system was not up to par. She had been gone for months. African parents didn't say much to us kids, so we just prayed. I was the older girl of three children. My older brother, who was born in the U.K., had somehow escaped the clutches of a dismal non-dream that would be the result of remaining in an undeveloped country; he left for the U.K. My younger sister was still in high school.

I wanted to be next, so I convinced my dad to let me take the SAT. He had no plans regarding how he'd pay the tuition, but he always figured it out. I sold him a story about how I could get a scholarship, so he let me take the SAT.

One evening, he returned and said to me, "You little minx, you did it!" I had since passed the SAT...but he had another surprise.

The letter was my admission letter to Georgia Southwestern State University. Oh my goodness! I was thrilled!

I suddenly didn't feel hot. I started making plans even though it was just an admission letter. That was how I started the next chapter of life. I was very sheltered, naïve, and trusting, and the only relationships I had observed up close were my parents' and those in my family dynamic.

I crossed the Atlantic, nevertheless, with an open heart and big, innocent eyes.

Perspective

One of the many inspirations for this book was connecting to the young girl with a heart full of dreams who somehow lost herself along the way. Maybe you can relate?

I have seen this happen countless times in life, and I cannot say it is for one reason or the other. I can only say it is our individual responsibility to connect with our young selves and ensure we are living out our dreams.

How do we do that during child-bearing years, or when we need to get higher education if we cannot afford it, or when there are physical obstacles, or so many other possible reasons?

My answer is not to put a time limit on it. Take it one step at a time. None of our dreams is small (I hope!), so we must create a sustainable plan to achieve the dreams. We must turn dreams into goals, and they must match our current situation. An example: if you cannot afford education, then you read, watch free videos, and talk to people. There are always ways to achieve your dreams. Get creative if you must, keep your eye out for resources, stay focused, and keep your eye on the end goal! You'll get there!

Discussion & Reflection Questions:

- Do you recognize yourself today?
- What are the dreams of your heart? What is stopping you?
- What can you do today to move toward your dreams?

Use the following journal pages to write out your thoughts.

CROSSING THE ATLANTIC

Imagine a little girl who grows up in Nigeria. Grows up in a house with her mom and dad. According to custom, Dad pays the bills, no questions asked. Dad gives Mom money for food and all household expenses: nannies, drivers, maids, etc. So, Mom is home, not working, given full support. The little girl sees all this and understands that's the way it's supposed to be.

Or is it?

Her dad attends her parent teacher conference, her mom threatens, "I'm going to tell your dad on you" for this or that, and she straightens up for the fear of his wrath. (Mom, he sometimes pretended for your benefit and came back and tickled us or gave us a treat.) Bottom line, her parents plan together. They are a team. Her dad buys her mom presents. They are happy. Their relationship has its own issues like most, but she sees that.

Fast forward twenty years. She comes to America and gets married with all this in her subconscious. In America, both parents work; both parents are involved in the kids' activities. There is no cheap labor. The mom does everything—in her case and in so many other cases that she sees. The moms are the ones who go to school for conferences and events and still have to work full-time.

She works, goes to activities, cooks dinner, cleans, schedules, and takes kids to their doctor's appointments, wakes up at night to feed the baby, goes back to work post-partum, (did you all get your first business idea when it was time to go back to work after having a baby?), and plays the roles of Mom and Dad. She does not understand this and is ill-prepared for this life.

Where is the life she was prepared for? How did this happen?

She didn't see it coming because she got caught up. She finally realizes that she messed up, and this was not what she thought marriage and raising children would be like. When she realizes this, she tries to make changes. She pushes back, tries to get her husband to step up, but he does not want to put in the work. Why should he disrupt his perfect life? Why should he choose a day to cook or provide dinner? Why should he leave this comfortable life?

I know a lot of people, especially immigrants, can relate to this. A coach I'm working with in my healing journey calls it "masculine wounded" or "feminine wounded." Masculine wounded is when a woman has been made to take on masculine roles or adopt masculine energy and is broken because that is not the way it's meant to be. (And vice versa for men, though this is not as common of a situation.) It causes trauma and makes us respond negatively to normal situations.

I am definitely wounded, and I bite whenever anyone tries to reach that part of me. We mixed everything up in the name of being millennials or baby boomers. We were trying to do something good by supporting our partners, but then the roles got mixed up—human nature kicked in—and now it's all a mess. I feel we should have had a rule book for how to be married and raise a family in the 21st century. Our parents tried to advise us, but their time was very different from ours. Personalities and consciences are on the decline. No one wants to be cheated, so it's all a game of survival of the fittest or the most thick-skinned, in this case.

I am still convinced that I will not conform to the bad habits of the world just to fit in. I have often struggled with acting or responding in a way that is not in my nature, like ignoring tasks in the home, pretending that I forget things so my partner would step up, and even allowing things to fall through the cracks. I would let things like bills fall, and I'd play on my partner's ego, knowing full well that he would not want the lights to go off.

But I just cannot be who I am not. An older family member once advised me to turn a blind eye to certain things in the home that wouldn't hurt me, like unwashed dishes or unwashed/unfolded laundry. But I just can't do it. I can't play the game of ignorance or weakness.

So, like my dad, I became a "your reward in is in heaven" woman. I had to forge on, cover my partner's inefficiencies, be strong for my kids, be a good wife, and be presentable.

It didn't work.

In my desperate effort to be all things to all people all of the time, I lost so much. I lost time. I lost my peace. But the most devastating thing is that I lost myself. I lost sight of the dream that little girl had of coming to the land of opportunity and becoming all you see on TV. I certainly think I did all the right things, but who am I kidding? TV is not reality. I did lose sight of my dreams, but I am getting back on track. I just got a little side-tracked.

I lost the perfect family I worked so hard and sacrificed for. I lost the husband and partner I endured with, hoping that one day the tables would turn. My children lost the chance of a complete family and have become statistics. Most of all, I lost time. And I can never get it back.

We need a manual! There has to be a better way. I will wait for a true partner who finishes my sentences, washes our clothes when I can't, understands their role in the home, does not make me the default for anything in the household, protects me, and wants what I want and vice versa.

I didn't come all this way not to live the "American Dream." Wait! As I write this, I realize there are many versions of the "American Dream." What's your American Dream?

Perspective

I have learned that only each individual knows what they want and what their threshold is. Share your dreams, limitations, and thresholds with your loved ones and watch how they respond and treat you.

Some may take advantage of the information, and some will respect it and use it to improve your relationship. We cannot stop living and dreaming because of a few bad experiences. We need to create our ideal family/relationships based on what and who we're involved with.

Finally, to my single or divorced friends, remember why you are where you are. Your life and time is not worth giving up your dreams and settling. If my experiences have taught me anything, it's that we all have a purpose and obligation on this earth. Let's find it!

Why is it so hard? Is it so hard to love thy neighbor or even the woman or man you promise to love and cherish before God and the court?

Discussion & Reflection Questions:

- Is there a lack of true love in this world?
- Is it so hard to love thy neighbor or even the woman or man you promise to love and cherish before God and the court?
- Are you scared to be labeled? Divorced, separated, etc.

Use the following journal pages to write out your thoughts.

PLAYING HOUSE

He would ghost me for days.

I did not grow up in a house where we kept malice, so I was not familiar with this behavior. It started even before we got married. We would argue over what I considered to be small things. Now when I look back, I see how monumental these things were in my marriage, and how it was being set up. We would argue—mostly around bedtime, ending maybe around 3 or 4 am—or I would assert myself on a point or a principle, and he would give me the silent treatment, knowing that I was unfamiliar with that form of warfare. Or any form of warfare in marriage or a loving relationship.

He would move to another room, and I would follow him, crying,

"What did I do to you?"

"Why don't you love me?"

"Why are you so mean?"

I could not understand it. (I was twenty-four. Don't even judge!) I was in a game within my own life, and I was not aware of it.

He would open the door to the other room after some time or not, and sometimes I would be strong enough to go to bed or go back to our bed, crying alone. The war was still going on. At this point, he had gained the upper hand. And he would wake up the next day still giving me the silent treatment. This would continue for days at a time.

After a couple of days, I found myself appealing to him to reconcile, but that would be one of my many mistakes. I was rarely ever in the wrong, but after this torture, I would doubt myself and question what even happened in the first place. We would go on with our day or lives and never really resolve the issue or learn how to fight fairly. (Yes, you will fight, so create rules of war.) This went on for at a least ten years. We had children in between. And life went on...

Another painful incident was when I was pregnant with my youngest, and we had relocated to Nigeria. His mom had come to stay with us. We still had so many quarrels, but this time, he would leave me in our room and stay up late talking with his mom and ignore me. I would have go to work, fight Lagos traffic (ask somebody! it's similar to LA traffic), deal with my racist South African bosses, field calls from the house about unnecessary groceries I'd have to pick up, deal with tutors calling me to complain about the kids not listening, have to stop at the neighborhood clinic because I had a mild malaria throughout my pregnancy that could not be aggressively treated because the medicine would affect the baby, and all sorts of other things...only to get home to him and his mom chilling, just having a conversation.

Oh! The irritation was unexplainable.

He would leave me in our room after I had dinner alone, and on top of it all, he was ghosting me. Yes, malice to him was saying "hi" and not really engaging with me, even when I asked him if he needed anything. And I was carrying this man's child.

After ten years, I was still a fool in love or life—you decide. This went on for at least two months until his mother got sick and passed away. At that point, I decided that I had had enough and decided to move back to the U.S., though other things contributed to my desire to return. I left, and he spoke to me the day before I left, but still...

PERSPECTIVE

What was really going on here was we were both trying to mold the other person or create our rules of engagement. This is common. But what I learned is that it really matters what is in the heart of the parties involved. I will say I was innocent and only asking for what I thought was right and fair. From my perspective, he was trying to subdue me, perhaps even control me, by mentally and emotionally strong-arming me. We all do it! Just in different ways.

Remember that whatever we call it—war, submission, love, familiarization, reconciliation—there must be rules and agreement of parties involved. You can still open your eyes and be in love!

Discussion & Reflection Questions:

- Have you been given, or do you give, the silent treatment in a close relationship?
- Have circumstances made you grow a thick skin to something? What is it? Why?
- Do you believe in rules of engagement in marriage/relationships?

Use the following journal pages to write out your thoughts.

A SHOULDER TO CRY ON

My girlfriend told me today that one of the ladies on the talk show *The Real* was discussing empaths and the kind of people they attract. The definition of an empath is "a person with the paranormal ability to apprehend the mental or emotional state of another individual." It sounds so grand and herculean. But it's not! It's sad and stressful.

Think of an empath as a sponge absorbing all of another person's emotions and processing all those emotions but never being squeezed dry. An empath with the wrong partner is doomed to a life of pain and a constant need to be understood and empathized with in return. The wrong partner will only take advantage of them.

Anyway, my girlfriend told me they were discussing this on *The Real*, and I was quite comforted by this news. It was more confirmation that I wasn't crazy or from another planet. This really hit home for me.

I remember chatting with a few of my girlfriends who are over forty, like me, about early marriage. These are women who I consider strong or at least stronger and more assertive than me. We laughed about how in the early stages of marriage, we would seek the face of our significant other. I would cry when I was hurt or when we argued, and that seemed to aggravate him more, not in a I'm-a-guy-I-don't-like-to-see-women-cry kind of way, but more of a you're-irritating-me-and-I-don't-want-to-deal-with-you way. He would leave the room, or I'd storm off and go in the closet or to another room, crying. Wishing that he would follow me and hold me and tell me it will be okay or just never let me leave the bed at all.

Wishful thinking on my part. Please! On many nights, I slept on that closet floor until the wee hours of the morning, or I spent the night in another room. He would have slept most of the night before he realized I wasn't there. And then he would come find me with a reluctant beckon to come back to bed. Or sometimes that gangsta just left me there. Remember the warfare I mentioned earlier? This war was about shifting and exerting power.

When talking to my friend (we talk a lot!), she mentioned how we have similar personalities but slightly different partners. We want to please everyone to make sure our partners and kids are happy. We may turn around and complain later, but we still bend over backwards to please others. If we do that unconsciously, why do we complain when they don't see us? How do you manage that? Do you spend a life not being yourself because you don't want to be taken advantage of? How does that look? It is a lonely, calculating place. Why do I have to pretend I don't see the trash overflowing, or leave the laundry unfolded, or not service my car because I want another human being to see me or notice?

Are they unwilling or unable? My therapist and I often wonder about this in my life.

I know many women who turn a blind eye to many things. Some even pretend to be weak or ignorant. And that works for them. Others just straight up call it out. They have the best marriages, in my opinion. Are they pretending, or has it become a lifestyle? Were they trained that way? Do their partners just love them so much? The equation is never equal as far as I am concerned, but I think that as much as we don't want to admit it, marriage, relationships, and partnerships need some level of strategy with love at the foundation.

I read an article about ten symptoms of a narcissist,* and the top symptom was "lacking empathy." When I think back on my relationships, I must admit that I have naturally attracted narcissists. I don't know how, but I have. When my current relationship ends, I am already scared of going out in the world and trying again because of my track record.

**See Glossary on page 270 for definition.*

Am I mature enough? Do I know what to look for? Do they spot me from a mile away? Do I send off a scent, like a dog in heat, saying, "Hey, look at me, you can totally brainwash me and take me for granted all day?" I, like every woman and man, want love and empathy and a shoulder to cry on.

Perspective

I don't care what games you have had to play to survive. I know for a fact that true love does not see you suffering and leave you. True love cannot see you crying and be unaffected. True love does not infight within its walls. True love gives you a shoulder to cry on—or does not let you cry at all.

Discussion & Reflection Questions:

- Have you had the opportunity to reflect and identify brokenness in your life?
- Do you blame that brokenness for unpleasant circumstances?
- Identify some of your most nurturing relationships.

Use the following journal pages to write out your thoughts.

MOTHERS AND BIG SISTERS

I am trying not to male-bash, but I am a female, so I can only speak from my experiences.

I find that girls who have very assertive mothers and have big sisters or a proxy, tend to make better choices.

Am I saying my mom is not assertive? Oh, no, not at all. She just was not assertive (or maybe I can say naïve) when it came to giving her child out in marriage. Both my parents were naïve and trusting, and there is nothing wrong with that—I love my parents, I would not change anything about them, and I know they are a true gift from the Lord to guide me—it's just that there's just something wrong with this crazy world.

I was the first of three to get married, the oldest girl. My mom was naïve and thought she was being civil when I was being courted. She probably did that because of her own experience in relationships, and especially hers with my dad. My parents have been married for forty-two years. Of course, they have had problems, but there is love at the core, and that's my final answer.

We had a great aunt who told my mom at the time of my courting to check out my partner's family, as was customary in Africa before marriage. But my parents were more liberal. They thought, *If that is who she loves, then we will accept him without checking anything.* Big mistake. I don't blame them at all for this because they wanted what I wanted and still support me unwaveringly today. We all have our regrets for not being more selective and critical, but we also did not want to fall into the category of those who put their future in-laws through hell. (Looking back, they needed a little jarring.) Well, I know why people check now.

Readers! Let your family give your partners hell. If they can stand the test and persevere, they are sincere.

A close friend brought my attention to the fact that I was missing a mentor or stronger woman close to my age. My mom played her role, but I needed someone who understood dating and the dynamics of my generations. She shared stories of her other friends and herself and how having a big sister or a very assertive friend who had a big sister really helped her. There is some validation a big sister role plays in giving you the confidence to say no and to help navigate what is acceptable and what is not.

We all need someone in our corner and in our generation that knows the workings of society. I think big sisters, whether biological or not, play that role.

Perspective

I had friends whose fathers would grill guys, and mothers who would tell the guys how this was their princess and jewel and how he had to take care of them. I thought they were doing too much.

I had friends in college who were not afraid to lose a suitor because he wasn't generous or did not show affection in public. I thought they were doing too much, but now I envy them because they knew what they wanted at such a young age.

Some of us (like me) are scared to turn suitors away or end up with wrong guy because he's accepting HIS child I'm carrying, or she's carrying my child, I don't want to be a single mom, he or she is cute, he or she checks off 70% of my list, everyone is getting married but me, they're just like I imagined they'd be in my fairytale, their body is banging, they are tall, I don't want to be the prettiest girl on the block with ten suitors today and none tomorrow. Most of us fall into this category. We settled!

I made a lot of my strongest decisions in life because I am a mother. I did not want my girls to grow up thinking the life I was portraying was normal, and that's how it should be. I didn't want my son thinking he was a mini lord in our home, and his sisters and I were there to serve him. I started hammering into them that the life we were living was not right. Mommies and daddies shouldn't behave like that. My son got it quickly, but my girls are still a work-in-progress because this dysfunction was our life for as long as they can remember. They are watching! We are the first and strongest influence in our children's lives.

Back to my mom and why I may be the way I am.

I grew up watching and learning from my mom, but I didn't end up with someone exactly like my dad. Plus, I only knew my dad growing up as a dad, not a husband.

I grew up watching my mom not having to ask for basic things, not having to fight for anything, with domestic staff to help her out, which never made me realize that my dad, like many African men, was not domesticated at all! He didn't have to be. He just had to provide the money. It was a different time, different country, and different people. But they were shaping a little girl's life.

Could they have done anything differently? I don't think so. I believe the Lord has us experience what we must to grow spiritually, but not everyone has to learn the hard way.

I wasn't prepared for the life I would go off to live across the Atlantic….

I went 'round and 'round about this chapter, but it's one that may seem like it's from a female perspective. I will update the perspective in the future when I find men to talk to me honestly.

Discussion & Reflection Questions:

- Do you have a big sister or brother, or someone like that in your life?
- Do you have a mentor?
- Are you outspoken about family norms with your children?

Use the following journal pages to write out your thoughts.

MY SOUL SISTER

Yes, my best friend needed her own chapter. This girl right here... wow!

People told me to stop talking to my best friend and see if that would make him happy. "Maybe then, he wouldn't have anything to complain about," they'd say. My best friend was sent to me by the Lord. I am glad I never considered anyone's advice to stop talking to her.

She scolds me when I over-spend but lets me know it's okay to spoil myself. She mothers me when she needs to and is a daughter to me when she needs me. She cares about me like a sister and converses with me like a friend. She is my rock, and I always pray that I can be even half of that to her. We had similar backgrounds with few differences but of similar socioeconomic status.

This girl is wise. She has the wisdom only an old woman can possess, but sometimes she also is vulnerable. I love our friendship. We define our rules of friendship as we go, in an unspoken agreement. I run to her after telling my mother any good or bad news in my life. We strategize together, brainstorm, laugh, plan, relax, and shop together. Of course, she has her own issues—just like anyone else—but her strength in handling them is admirable.

When the issues in my marriage were at a peak, she said to me, "I would rather be here for you now and let your husband be mad at me than leave you alone to please him. If you guys reconcile one day, I am okay to stay away." Wow! Who does that? I don't even know if I would do that if I were in her shoes. Do you agree she is a Godsend? Why did he not like her? Well...due to the fact that he was listening to my private conversations, he heard some of my gossiping sessions with her, and he also saw what she was to me: a support that he could never be.

(I know...unnerving, right? I asked a cyber investigation company to scan my devices, and I found spyware on my phone and my laptop. What's sad is that it could be an actual cyber-crime, or my ex's doing. I honestly would never know.)

Our friendship was threatened by my ex through false accusations and blackmail. But we stayed friends. I was told that she could not come to my fortieth birthday party. It was her or my husband at the time. I ignored him and invited her. I was told horrible things about her, but I knew they were false—just a way for him to push her away from me.

I often wondered if she was told horrible things about me, and she admitted to me recently that she *was* told things about me by my ex-husband. He feigned seeing her off to her car on my fortieth birthday to apologize to her for the ultimatum (so he told me), but he actually told her horrible things about me. She refused to tell me what, but she did say something that he also said to my dad during a reconciliation conversation: "You don't know her." This was to plant a seed of doubt in their minds. He said this to my father and my best friend. Wow!

I was accused of running to her first with my problems or with good news. This accusation was right: I did. I ran to my best friend in my darkest times because she welcomed me with open arms, rejoiced with me, and cried with me, and she also cautioned me and supported me no matter what.

My friend is still here for me now. We still talk almost every day. I am so grateful and glad I have her. We give each other advice, laugh together, agree to disagree, and just have a blast. I love her like my sister.

Perspective

This essay is about support and true friendship. If your story is like mine or you have experienced half or even a quarter of what I have experienced, you need a good support system. My family has been a great support system to me, but greatest of all is the support of a non-blood relative.

I have been around the block. I often attract friendships that are based on competition and envy or parasitic friendships. But this friendship has been different. It's been a Godsend.

Imagine not having to worry about what you share with someone, the comfort of knowing that this person has your back and does not covet what you have. A friend who is confident and content with themselves and does not agree with you all the time to make you feel better about your bad decisions. What I am describing could be your girlfriend or guy friend or sister or brother, and if you're lucky, even your spouse.

Ahh, spouse...that would be nirvana. I pray you find that kind of partnership. I am still looking forward to that kind of love, but no one can take the place of my soul sister. She gets me!

Do you have a friend you can trust and who has your back? If you are going through anything like me, you need one.

Discussion & Reflection Questions:

- Do you have a friend you can trust who also has your back?
- Has your trust been betrayed by a friend?
- Do you have several friends for several purposes?

Use the following journal pages to write out your thoughts.

UNSPOKEN AGREEMENTS

Have you ever felt like, "Wait, how did I become the default?" I have!

It's not anyone's fault. I feel like communication and agreement is key in any relationship. Later on I will talk about how couples must talk and agree on their finances, but we also must agree on how we're going to run our homes and on who will do what in the house. No one wants to feel like a default. There are real feelings at play here.

I am one of those people who is always ready to do things even before being asked. I'm impatient. I love to help. I also grumble and complain when I am not appreciated. When my best friend asks me, "Who asked you to do this?" I stop my complaining and think, and that's when it occurs to me: I wasn't asked. I just jumped the gun and did it as usual.

My husband would say on a Tuesday, "Hmmm, we should clean the house. It's dirty." And like clockwork on Saturday morning, I would wake up before anyone and start cleaning. Fully expecting everyone, most of all him, to join me. By noon, I would be fuming. Did my husband tell me to wake up on Saturday and clean? No! People who like to take advantage of others love people like me. I just do stuff because it needs to be done.

There's also a flip side to this unspoken agreement when running a household. You and your partner must agree on who will do what. This is important. If you are like me and you don't ask, then you will be the default for everything. You must talk about everything. You have to have a system in your house. If you and your partner work full-time, then you cannot be a housewife and do all the things a housewife does. If you ARE a housewife, you will need a break from the kids or cooking or whatever. We all need a break. We don't want to feel like our roles are not appreciated. You need to know who cooks, and if the person who cooks gets tired or burnt out, they need to be able to speak up, and their cry for help needs to be received with love. If the person who takes the kids to the games gets tied up, they need to know their partner will step up. So even though I say you need to talk about everything, you also need to know your partner and feel when they need you.

This is key. I had a conversation with a friend recently on an Instagram Live, and he said to me, "My wife and I have been together long enough to just know when we need each other." He continued by saying they did not have to talk about or make any agreements. This is because there is a mutual unspoken agreement of love between them. They feel each other's emotions and know each other well enough to step up when needed. It's common sense, y'all.

But what about my situation? I had also been with my partner long enough for us to know each other. It does not matter. You have to look at the type of partner you have. Some people just don't see you or hear you or pretend they cannot see you or hear you. Some people are content to let you do all you will do like in my case. As long as you act like a darn jack-in-the-box, they will let you. So study your partner and create a formula that works for you. I know some who feign weakness or being a damsel in distress, and it has worked for them. Oh, but don't be like me and show who you can be, then try to switch up to damsel in distress or be physically unable to. It won't work. You have already made your bed, and so you must lie in it. It takes a very special person or an act of God to turn a situation like mine around. I was not successful.

Let me give you an example with my husband and then my kids.

Let's say I go and get my hair done; ladies, you know how long that takes. I leave at 7 am on a Saturday and come back at 2 pm. Keep in mind that the kids are not home alone. Their dad is home, too. At this point, I hadn't started a schedule with my kids on who does dishes weekly. So, when I walk into the house, I see that the house is a mess!

Dishes in the sink, kitchen in disarray, and then—after my bellowing at my kids that I'm not their maid (I'm really mad at my husband for not telling them to clean up)—my youngest comes up to me and says she's hungry.

I totally lose it. My husband innocently comes out of his office, wondering if I've gone mad. I am mad, all right…but mad as in furious! This is a pet peeve for me, and why wouldn't I share it with you, just in case you can relate? Anyway, what happened here was that we didn't talk. Nothing happens after these episodes happen in my home, and because I get so angry, my husband and I never talk about it.

Please, my dear readers! Talk about stuff. Agree. Don't have unspoken agreements. We should have agreed and talked about it the first ten times it happened and agreed what we would do. My example might be a bit extreme, but I think we need to agree on stuff. It is the key to a functioning home. Like my husband would say, "division of labor."

Let's talk about realignment. Remember I said you should have the conversations, but you also have to realign when there are major life events or changes. Communicate!

Perspective

People still ask me today if I asked for help. Really? Of course I did! I asked for help repeatedly. I examined the results and asked a different way. I even pretended to be unable to do things, and they just fell through the cracks.

Ask for what you want, but the person must receive it and act on it. Don't assume your partner knows or they will just read your mind and do what you need. You should talk about it if you are with someone who will not pick up on your feelings or cues. It didn't work for me when I tried to create agreements in my marriage because we didn't have two willing participants who were going to hold up their end of the agreement. I have recently talked to some friends who said that talking and agreeing how they will function in their homes has worked for them. All they needed was to talk to their partners and let them see their pain or discomfort with the situation. I am happy about that and happy that I was able to help my friends reach that point and overcome trivial issues that can become not so trivial with time. There is some growing to do. We are all human; people will slack off. Men need you to repeat without getting angry. Know your man. Before you get angry, confirm your assumptions before you go HAM on them.

I shared with them that it does not happen overnight, but the integer in the equation is always a willing partner who has some atom of love for them. They found it in their partners. Some had to dig deeper and eventually found it. I was not so lucky, but I am not licking my wounds. I am writing so I can help others, and I am looking forward to finding a love like I read about and dream about.

"Don't apologize for opening your eyes."

—SE

Discussion & Reflection Questions:

- Do you think that love still exists for you if you have been hurt?
- Does your partner wait until you are too far gone before they listen?
- What was the straw that broke the camel's back in any of your relationships?

Use the following journal pages to write out your thoughts.

STRENGTH IN NOT SETTLING

Is marriage now a transaction?

I wonder what people's idea of marriage is.

When I was growing up, marriage was what my dad and mom had. In the evenings she would wait up for him to come back from work before she would eat dinner. I'd be waiting to get a piece of his chicken, our family danced to Michael Jackson...oh, just the ease of it all. Things were much easier when I was growing up, or maybe that's what my parents wanted me to see. Then again, were they supposed to have serious conversations about life with a seven-year-old?

I will admit that I have judged and gossiped about the same women I now admire for their strength. In my culture, it takes strength to ignore all the urgings, pressure, insinuations, mockery, and so on that come with not getting married at the perceived appropriate age.

The truth is that these women know what they want and are not willing to settle until they get it.

I spoke to a single friend named Ope, and she said to me, "I learnt early on that happiness doesn't come from people or possessions." Plus, her parents had been together for forty-eight years, and they just seemed to be going through the motions. Her happiness comes from within.

Wow! What a knowledge of self at such a young age. I envy her even more now. I definitely went through the motions and did what was expected without once questioning it. My friend Ope also said she would never give up being single to end up in marriage that made her worse off than she was as a single woman. How do people even articulate life to that point? Wow! I was really naïve or something. This wise woman also went on to say, "Once I freed myself from what society expected of me, I was good." This just gives me goosebumps because I didn't even think this deeply. I just went with what society dictated. I am learning so much on this journey.

I still don't know what the big hurry was for me. I was unconsciously checking boxes. Fear made me jump to get married to one of the first people to ask me to marry him. It's weird when I think of it now. I really don't know what got into me. Looking back, I think it was fear. Fear that no one else would come calling.

Why would I think that? I was and am a beautiful woman with so much to offer. But if I didn't believe it, how did I expect others to? This speaks to my self-confidence and knowledge of self. I was not as bold as my friends I once gossiped about, and look at me now, seventeen years later, divorced.

I recently spoke to a young lady named Rolake, and she talked to me about the importance of values, principles, and beliefs. She spoke about how these values had affected her choices. She is still single, and she is thirty-one years old. The old me would have taken a second look to find fault in her, but today I admire her for sticking to her guns. Rolake is beautiful and has a lot to offer but not to the highest bidder.

Growing up in Africa, a very traditional and idealistic continent, there was little opportunity to mix with people of different classes, backgrounds, and beliefs socially. It just wasn't going to happen because the opportunities didn't present themselves. Now, crossing the Atlantic to the land of opportunity was a whole different story. In America, there was no class consciousness, especially for immigrants who had to collaborate to understand the workings of the system. Americans are liberal compared to Africans.

Rolake shared how she, like many middle- to upper-class Africans, came to America for a higher education with the full intention to go back home to Africa. No one plans to stay, but one thing leads to another.

She found herself dating and mixing with people of different backgrounds as she went about her life. She started getting close to her supposed marrying age and started getting the pressure from family members, the odd comment here and there about how she was always a bridesmaid and never a bride. She was only human. She entertained the thought, but the prospects were just not worth it. The African men were westernized, the American men were not African. All these conditions and stereotypes in the back of her mind...the pressure was so much for her. She almost married the wrong guy once, but she found out just before plans were finalized that he just did not share her values and beliefs. So, she called it off, to the horror of her family and his. I applaud her! I would never have been bold enough, but what's a lifetime of unhappiness compared to one bold move?

Rolake continues to wait for her Boaz* and is now open to a wider variety of men because she realizes that her happiness is more important than other people's expectations. Lucky her!

Another friend of mine, Christina, who is now married, waited until she was thirty-two to get married. That's long by African standards. She spent most of her dating years in Africa. She came from a very wealthy extended family, but her parents had been forced to retire early due to corruption and economic destabilization in Africa. So, they lived in the boonies of the city. She had lots of wealthy family who tried to hook her up with their friends, but she didn't encourage it because she felt no one was going to come and visit her where she lived. Christina's parents were also very active in their church, and people came from far and wide to worship there. This was another avenue for her to meet eligible bachelors. She soon also found out that because your parents go to the same church does not mean you share their values. So, there were some failed relationships there too. She just gave up and focused on her career. She soon met her Boaz and is living happily with her family in America.

**See Glossary on page 270 for definition.*

Perspective

Christina shared from her experience that very few people are willing to love without an agenda these days. That is so true. There are no knights in shining armor out there just willing to sweep someone off their feet. Everyone wants to know what you have to offer. People also treat you differently based on your and your family's socioeconomic status. You find that husbands respect in-laws with money more and treat their wives better to avoid the wrath or shunning of their wealthy, influential father-in-law. Both women and men tread carefully with more influential families. Women elevate their social status by hanging out at elite locations to meet the right kind of guy and fight tooth and nail to keep a good catch. I don't blame them. Marriage and relationships are moving away from love, God's design for marriage, and shared values.

I have always been a strong believer in the idea that "love conquers all." I believe that all the scenarios painted above can be overcome by true love. Call me a romantic.

Our parents don't tell us outright that the partner you choose should come from a family that comes from a similar background as you. It is important. I am not speaking here only about class or money. I am talking about values and experiences that shape positive outcomes. What do I mean by this? You cannot expect someone who grew up in a home without a father to know how to be a good or bad father because there was no firsthand example, but then you can commend someone who vows to get support and learns to be the best father they can.

Ope's thoughts about happiness from within really got me thinking. She is absolutely right. We seem to think that being married is some sort of societal badge.

Rolake told me when we spoke that she has come across a lot of guys who come from a "mindset of lack."

"It is dog eat dog out there," she said.

People are not willing to give without some assurance of payback. It is survival of the fittest. I listened to her and honestly, I had never seen it like that, but she was very right. People are no longer willing to love and reciprocate love as the foundation of every relationship. I find that people who just leave themselves unprotected and unbiased and just love, get burnt, even charred to the point where they no longer recognize themselves.

So, when these ladies and gents are asked why they won't settle? I don't blame them for asking, settle for what? Did you settle? Did you wait for the right guy or gal? Were you given a second chance at love?

I always ask myself now, what was the hurry? Did I really understand the sanctity of marriage? I think I did understand the sanctity, but I think I did not know myself enough and I was not exposed enough.

This might be a bit left field for you, but I truly believe that I was supposed to get married and experience this pain and failure to realize my purpose. I believe it. But do you believe in this kind of fate? Will you accept it for yourself?

Discussion & Reflection Questions:

- Did you give into pressure and settle?
- Did you know yourself before marriage?
- How did you know he or she was the one?

Use the following journal pages to write out your thoughts.

LEADERSHIP OR CONTROL

I have written many chapters about this and deleted them. I am struggling about this message in particular because I am torn between talking about control and abuse, but in fact control is a form of abuse. It is a form of forcing our will on others and in turn depriving them of their free will.

So, I will talk about control and help you understand how it escalates to abuse.

I've been searching for definitions of a leader online, and I found a source that claims this: a leader in a home leads by example, is fearless, honors others, does what's right, not what's easy, inspires, and finds goodness and beauty in everyone and everything.

I was also looking online for a definition of control. One source stated that control is the ability to direct the actions of someone or something or an action or method that limits the amount or growth of something.

You know I only talk about what I have experienced or heard of. I have been talking to a male friend of mine, and he married someone twelve years younger than him. They got married about ten years ago and had four children back to back. His wife was new to the U.S. when they married and didn't really have a chance to spread her wings when they got married and started to build their family. My friend is a doctor who is very hard working and provides for his family, and his wife has also managed to build a career for herself.

Now! Ten years later, my friend shared with me that he is getting older and wants to live his life differently, meaning that he wants to be more pious. And his wife is at the stage where she finally has raised her kids to a point where she can spread her wings. Live her life. The first time my friend complained to me, I told him that I wished my ex-husband had a woman like me to tell him the truths of life. I have always ensured that my communication with my friend was appropriate and that if his wife ever saw our correspondence, she would not feel betrayed by another woman. Anyway, when he complained to me, I told him that what he and his wife were going through was normal and he should be patient and see it from her point of view. He was adamant that she wanted to live a life of sin.

What life of sin, I asked? I told him to let me guess. She wanted to have brunch with the girls (he probably didn't approve of the girls), buy the latest designer bags, go to a lounge or club with the girls (she even invited him to join her), start to spend her money like a grown woman, etc.

He asked me, "Do you hide in my basement and listen?"

I told him I didn't. I am just a woman, and we all do it when approaching forty or when we feel we have given enough. I advised him to let her be and love her through this stage.

He wanted her to have Bible study every night and be on the same spiritual level as him, but I warned that he had to lead by example and show her who he served and what made him different instead of alienating her.

He didn't listen, and now they are talking about divorce. This could have been avoided.

He was and is not leading. He is controlling.

Another common story is that of some foreign tribes that bring young women (not underage) to the U.S. under the pretext of changing their lives and giving them a piece of the American dream. They dazzle them in their poor countries and bring them here and marry them, and the girls are malleable to some extent because they are young, and women adapt easily. The women have all intentions to marry and build a home with these men…but the men are usually not as affluent as they portray, and by the time the women realize this, it's too late. They send them usually to nursing school and support them through school, barely, and then the women graduate and become nurses. These men expect retribution for supporting their own wives. When the women start to push back or realize the game, it becomes ugly and abusive. Many in the state of Texas and recently Florida have lost their lives to domestic abuse tracing back to these types of beginnings.

Again, is the man leading or controlling? He is using someone's child as a retirement plan, in my humble opinion.

I know the guys are getting mad at me, so let's talk about the inverse. We can take any of the two situations above, or just even a guy who means well and marries a younger girl, an older girl, or just a girl. They build their family, and the man leads and does his bit, but he has married the devil herself or a distant cousin of the devil or just a manipulative human being. Many women are broken due to trauma from the past or just selfish.

So, question…are some women blessed with good men, or do they create their good men? I often wonder. I have always felt like my ex would have been a different man with the right type of woman who knew how to get what she wanted, but then he also always told me he knew what he wanted in a woman. I should have hightailed it then and there.

Back to my story. I see several men who do everything right and try to build a family, but the women are abusive to them, selfish, or just not ready. I have seen many men stay and play dual roles. I have seen some seek solace outside the home. I have seen men accept their fate. And I have seen some men leave. As a woman, I cannot relate and would probably be biased, but I say it can't be as bad as the fate of a woman.

There's also the case of subtle control where, during dating, the guy asks his girl where she is. He wants a play-by play of her movement. She thinks it's cute, until one day she challenges him on it jokingly, and he plays it off until he doesn't play about it again; he actually wants to know her every move.

A few months later, he starts to comment on her clothes and how she dresses too cheaply and how she needs to dress sophisticated. So, he starts buying her clothes. She still thinks it's cute. After a year of dating, he replaces her whole wardrobe. She starts to wear only things he buys her and goes only where he wants her to go. He even takes her around when they're not working, and she thinks it's nice that he always wants to spend time with her, but she slowly stops seeing her friends.

He is in finance, so he starts helping her budget and save her money. When it's time to get married, he tells her "their" vision for the wedding. She goes along with it.

Do you see how this situation has escalated? And if it continues to escalate—which it might—it could very well go from controlling to abuse.

I personally craved leadership and partnership, but I got control. It is sad that a marriage or relationship like most things now is also about survival of the fittest, or survival of the baddest. I like arrogance in a guy. I think it's cute. But can an arrogant person be humble and lead? I'm still trying to figure out the balance, and I'll definitely share once I get it right.

Perspective

My ex-husband always told me that he didn't understand what I meant when I said he wasn't letting me be myself, and I never had a response after that. Now that I am on my own, I can see how he stifled me. I would like to say that he didn't do it on purpose and that it was just out of habit and my allowing him, but I don't know. I would still like to give him that benefit of the doubt.

All of us are broken in one way or another, but we must be mindful of imposing our will on others. You cannot say because you are the man of the house, your will is paramount. Will is not ours to give. It is a gift from the Lord.

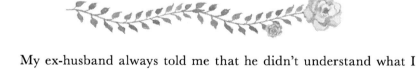

So, when given a choice between a controller or a leader, I will choose a leader every time. I want to be a leader and lead by example.

Let's be mindful that our control does not turn into abuse or take us away from our intentions, assuming they are good.

Discussion & Reflection Questions:

- Can you tell the difference between leadership and control? Write about an example in your life.
- Do you believe control may not be abuse in some cases? Why?
- Do you believe good women/men are shaped or born like that?

Use the following journal pages to write out your thoughts.

GRACE AND EASE

Some said to me, "You made it look so easy. That's why he doesn't understand." Others said, "You kept quiet and took it for too long." Still others said, "We didn't know you were going through everything you went through because you carried yourself with so much grace."

It was almost like people I called my friends were saying I was doing just fine, so why now?

I had painted such a perfect picture that no one believed me. Even as I write, I still find myself on the defensive, trying to convince fellow women, wives, and mothers that I was dying inside, and I made the best decision for myself. I almost felt like I was in the doctor's office, having to embellish or start bleeding to convince someone to give me meds.

I am doing much better now and find myself needing less and less to defend myself. It's not that the calls, flying monkeys,* or conversations have stopped. I'm getting stronger in my resolve to try life a different way.

One thing I am realizing is that I have hundreds of complaints or issues, and everyone chooses which one of my many issues they feel strongly about. Can you imagine people picking apart your pain? Some would say, "He should definitely pay the mortgage" or "He shouldn't have listened to your calls." It felt like they were minimizing all my other pain.

I told my mom that I felt like a prostitute selling my story, and no one believed me because I took the money and spent it.

**See Glossary on page 270 for definition.*

I also told my friend that I felt like I had not had my day in court. Can't you hear me? Why did I really think or need people to hear me when I didn't look like I had anything going on? I painted such a perfect picture. I have to forgive myself for that. Was I doing the right thing? You are supposed to protect your marriage, right?

Perspective

Don't hide things now that you may want people to see later. It is like hiding evidence in a murder case where you are the defendant. If you do, no one will hear you. This stems from not being yourself or not being able to be yourself. Either way, you have to take control and responsibility for your life. No one should be able to silence you, and no one who loves you should want you to hide your pain or live it.

Partnership is about freedom to be yourself and how all parts make a whole. I felt I was keeping the family together while being a supportive and good partner, but I was not free. There was no grace or ease in what I was doing. I was suffering in silence. Granted, families have things they don't want to share with others, but not everything is a secret or should be hush-hush. The advice not to share your secrets is valid to some extent because there are people who don't wish you well. The advice not to share your pain is also valid because there are those who thrive on the pain of others, but you can only learn who those are by experience.

Take a chance.

Friends! Have a confidant or two. Have an accountability partner, have someone who can tell you you're being foolish. Learn to tell the difference between those who wish you well by experiencing. Live your life, be yourself. Don't hide your truth because when you're ready to tell it, it may be heard as a lie. Please don't get me wrong—it is not about what people think. It's just about how you should go through life.

No man is an island. You must have one person. It could be your momma! I brought my mom in too late. Don't be like me.

My perspective also reflects where I was the day I wrote the paragraph above, but today, one month after I realize that, the true strength is not giving a darn! Hide, don't hide, tell, don't tell. YOLO (you only live once). What if you caught this virus now? Would you care what people thought of you or be scared to feel your pain?

Discussion & Reflection Questions:

- Do you hide your marital issues?
- Do you have a confidant/accountability partner?
- Are you carrying a big burden and pretending?

Use the following journal pages to write out your thoughts.

Perspective on Perspective:

A girl at my hairdresser said, "Men have no idea what we go through because we make it seem so easy to the extent that they get overwhelmed."

Another one said she doesn't know why she carries so much, but she knows now that she made a mistake because when she asks for help, she gets a blank, unsympathetic stare. Not his fault! She couldn't wait for him to wrap his head around helping her, so she got up and did it like usual. You know what I mean—you do it too! That's your fault.

Wait....

Another one of my divorced friends said she also never let her ex-husband make decisions for her kids because of an experience from her childhood, and she didn't realize it until years after the divorce.

Her mom had allowed her dad to decide about her school, and she saw her mom not fight for her when she thought she should have fought. As a little girl, that marked her, and she unconsciously resolved to fight for her kids even if they didn't need her to fight. She ended up fighting the wrong battles and never let her ex-husband make decisions about their children.

When I was teaching my kids to wash dishes, someone told me not to fuss over how clean the dishes were, how much soap or water they wasted, or how they left the sink. That was sound advice. When we ask for help, we cannot dictate how the help is given.

MY SWARM

I have often been asked how my loved ones felt about what I had gone through and was going through. I can't ever say for sure how they felt, but I will try to understand and explain how I think they felt.

My Mother

I called my mom almost every day when I returned to the U.S. after my wedding. We had guests staying with us, and I found it strange that we would have anyone staying with us when we were newlyweds. My husband would talk late into the night with his cousin, and I would be left alone in my bed. Where was the fairytale? Well, sis, no fairytale for you. You lived with him before marriage. That's what you get.

Oh lawd—sorry Mom and Dad. The cat is out of the bag. Yes, I lived with my husband before marriage and all that comes with it.

I would call my mom crying and tell her I was done, and she would say, "No, don't say that, it's only been a month, what would people say?" and she would cheer me up and tell me some of her horror stories in marriage, but the difference was it was other people that hurt her in her early marriage, not my dad. I didn't catch on to that.

When I opened up to her in 2016—we're now in July of 2020 in the middle of rising COVID cases in America, the day after we had 70,000 cases in one day—she did what any mother would do. She asked if I wanted her to talk to my husband or tell my dad to talk to my husband, and I said no. I gave one of those, "Mom, I only need you to listen, not fix it" responses. She didn't like it, but she respected me. I was happy because I had one more person other than my best girl to share my feelings with. I didn't want to overburden my best friend.

When my mom saw things were not getting better and my husband walked out on the family while she was visiting, she knew things were out of hand. She continued to listen, support, and advise.

When it all came out, she was angry at herself for not letting me react, for giving me patience, and for giving my husband the benefit of the doubt. She was his strongest advocate, and he turned on her the most. It was ugly.

My mom, I believe, is still waiting for her day of yelling. She probably wants to go all gangsta on him and tell him his life history, like, everything.

Mothers want to protect, and I didn't let my mother do that for me. I robbed her of her chance to be a mama bear. Instead, I painted this perfect picture because I wanted her to accept my husband as her son, and she did. I should have allowed her to come to her own conclusions and should not have protected him so much. Maybe I wouldn't be in this mess. I should have let my mom be a mother to me. Instead, I shared my mother with him and put her in a very difficult situation.

She was nice and welcoming and treated him like her son, and he turned on her and disrespected her for it. He blamed her for standing up for me when she finally did and tried to turn me against my own mother.

It comes back to lying and painting a perfect picture because you will be the canvas that is framed with the picture. Trapped, and your loved ones won't be able to reach you.

My Father

I'm a daddy's girl even though our relationship is extreme. We are either in love or going at each other, but I'm still a daddy's girl. I remember a romper I had that said, "My heart belongs to daddy." I believed it and still believe it until this day. My daddy is my hero, and

I trust him completely. He was the first man I loved, and I know that if I fall, he will catch me. He taught me what a man should be and it has worked for me and against me.

My mom and I often hide things from my dad because he can be a bit extreme and he has a bad temper. So, when I started sharing things with my mom after twelve years of marriage, we still didn't tell him.

When he found out, he was very upset. His little girl had been hurt and not been taken care of as promised. He felt betrayed and deceived. He recalled when he had been asked for my hand in marriage and how he had warned that he had a very small family, and how my mom had difficult pregnancies. See…I was born premature, and they were not sure I would make it, but I did. My dad was not playing!

My dad was and is angry about being tricked and deceived into believing his little girl was being taken care of, only to find out that was not the case at all. I believe he is angrier than I am. I still have not reached the point of anger. I am not sure why. Maybe because I am still confused.

My dad told me he wants to get him in a boxing ring with no rules and box him. Ha.

All fingers point back to me again when it comes to Dad. I did not let my family in. I understand that not everything in marriage is to be discussed or shared outside marriage, but why lie and protect the façade? I don't know…it's what I thought best at the time.

My father intervened when he was briefed, about a year before our separation. He did not behave how I expected and how I wanted him to react. I wanted him to be angry and rake my husband over hot coals, but there were my mistakes again, coming back to bite me.

I had painted such a perfect picture of my marriage, so all the information was coming from left field and was overwhelming to my dad after so much time. He felt it couldn't be so bad if I had endured. Also, since I had never allowed my parents to intervene in my marital affairs, they had no ground to stand on. My husband made promises to my dad during his intervention, so he would back off and he did.

Many months later he did not live up to his promises as usual and we separated.

My dad felt fooled and betrayed.

My father could not fight for me because he didn't have ammunition, and he couldn't protect me because I had left everyone exposed by manipulating the situation to maintain my façade.

The one thing that gave my father ammunition was when my marital issues started to affect my health. He had dealt with anxiety and hypertension for many years, and finally he could relate.

He has never backed down again!

My Sister

Little sis. I know this may be hard for you to read, but we did have a rough time and it seemed like it all got better after the separation.

My little sister is six years younger than me. She lived with me for about two years when she moved from Nigeria to America. During that time, she observed my family dynamic up close. I was still able to hide some stuff…but not everything.

I had a lot of unexplained issues with my sister in the last five years, but I did not understand the root of our issues.

My sister got married a little late by our standards, but she took her time to ensure she did not end up with someone like I did, or so I think. You see, having observed my predicament up close, she was able to see the things she didn't want to do or wouldn't accept.

Once she got married, I believe her admiration for me as a big sister was affected because of what I was putting up with. She felt I had lost myself and could no longer be that big sister she looked up to. Though I may be wrong, it is what I believe happened. She couldn't understand why I stayed and why she should look up to or seek advice from someone like me. This is my interpretation of what happened to us during that time. She recently shared with me that she didn't understand why I was being treated unfairly when I worked so hard after all we had overcome to come to the land of opportunity. She didn't feel it was fair for me to carry so much when I was in a marriage. She just couldn't understand it.

As soon as I separated from my husband, our relationship changed, and she became more open. She told me how she did not like to see me all those years going through so much pain and mistreatment. She felt like fighting for me, but she knew she couldn't, so she stayed away. This affected our relationship and put her in a difficult situation. She didn't feel comfortable visiting me and was never comfortable in my home. I never really understood until my situation changed.

My sister wished there was a law against what I went through so my husband could be held in contempt. She is very practical and maybe too practical. Everything is black or white for her. No grey. Although I am not 100% certain that my husband was the cause for our issues, I know he did not help our relationship. It was like a torment for my sister that her only family here in the States was enduring so much. Who would she look up to? Who would advise her? Definitely not the one who needs advice herself.

My consolation regarding my sister is that I feel I was there for her to look up to, maybe not be proud of, but to look up to. She was able to see marriage through me and know what she wanted and what she didn't want. She was able to choose well and find someone who truly loved her and had her back. For that I am happy and don't feel bad about this one result of my marriage.

My Brother

We call him the diplomat of our family. He is my older brother. He also came to visit with me and stayed for about three months. He observed some things but kept them to himself. He often asked me during his stay if I was okay, and I always said I was fine, but he wasn't blind. He respected my responses and didn't push. Whenever I opened up to him about things, he always offered very practical and rational explanations to me. He always sees the best in everyone.

I shared many things with my brother, but I think what really got him was when I told him my phone had been bugged. He could not believe it and could not stand the audacity. Why would someone even do that? Was his sister so bad? He responded to the threat to my personal safety. That was what got him riled up.

After I shared that, he became my confidant and the one I would go to when I wasn't seeking harsh advice or advice that would require me to do anything out of the norm for me. He sympathized with me but remained in shock. He is not a very extreme person and gets angry only once in three years, so he remains a source of support, and I assume he has not really shown me how he feels because he does not want to make matters worse. I told you he's a diplomat, right? I shared with you how everyone reacts differently to parts of my story, but I had to live it all. Well, my brother reacted to safety and the need to protect me. He had seen some traits in my husband that he just could not understand and had shared them with me, gently cautioning me to adjust my behavior for the situation I was in. But I didn't do much about it. He advised me to discuss issues when they came up, and I did just that, but I didn't get the responses I was expecting.

My brother was and still is my voice of caution and reason, but he will carry that reason and caution anywhere for me.

My brother wants what I want.

I wish my husband would see reason.

I think it's important to point out that out of my close inner circle, only my sister and my BFF live in the same country as me. That being said, my brother cannot be physically present to protect me and stand in for me as a brother should, but he will if he had to. Thankfully, there was never the need. I love having someone with my brother's temperament around me because sometimes you need some rationality. He does not get emotional and gives me sound advice. As I said, he is always concerned about my safety and that of my children's. All said, he will buy a ticket and fly from Europe to my rescue at the first cry.

My BFF

My best friend has mastered the art of pushing past stuff. I honestly don't know where she stuffs things. She says it's from experience, I say it's a sixth sense. She has a very busy life like me, and life throws stuff at her too, but unlike me, she sees it coming.

She always experiences stuff with her family before me. It's so funny. She could be telling me a story of an experience about one of her kids, and two years later, one of my kids would go through the same thing. We would just laugh. I confided in her years before I talked to my mom. She was always careful to provide the advice I was ready to accept or she felt I could handle. Her concern was my well-being, and her prayer was that my husband would open his eyes to the jewel he had. She is Catholic, and apart from being Catholic, she just doesn't advocate for divorce, or she never advocated for it in my case.

Her thoughts on my situation? She is probably still in shock. In Africa, we call it "moving the goal post." When you think you finally got it, they move the goal post. I shared many of my thoughts on getting my husband to see reason with her, but she never gave direct advice, now that I think back. She would just always be there to listen and share a few details of her own experiences. I did many things that I thought would wake him up. He always promised change but never made changes. When I threatened to sell our house that he loved so much and showed off to his friends, maybe he would take me seriously that I was drowning. No, no change! Or when I actually put the sign up? No. When I actually sold it? No again. When I asked for a separation? No again. While we were separated and he traveled to bring back a fortune for us to start over? He didn't bring back anything—just stories and excuses.

That's the shock I believe she is still in and can't recover from. But she pushed past it as is her way to support me. She feels like I have been treated unfairly but shared with me that she had still been holding out hope for a reconciliation. She still thought that surely he was just going through a phase.

Shocked that he didn't fight more for me or his family, for not showing up and doing the things I asked for. Shocked that he would sit and watch his family go without a fight or a plan on getting them back. An actual plan, not words. Real change. She feels bad that he didn't show up and step up, that he didn't make immediate changes, but instead quarreled and alienated us.

My best friend feels like she could put our friendship aside and talk to him like he was a stranger on the street that made her angry. Like really go in on him.

She would always say, "I am so sorry that you are going through this. You have a beautiful heart, you are gorgeous, you're hardworking, you do more than I could ever dream of doing, and I know if you had the emotional support, you would still be in your marriage doing whatever it took, but you were given no choice."

She understands me and is just the friend I needed in my life at this time. We all need someone when the going gets tough. My BFF understood what I needed and walked through every step with me. There was never a time I needed her that she wasn't there. I know there were times she wanted to knock sense into me, but she loved me through it. What I learned from her was how to focus on the changes I needed to make on myself because those are the changes you can control.

My Best Cousin

This one recently got in trouble again for the hundredth time defending family. My cousin loves family and protects hers like a mama bear. We are the same age, but she has always been there for me. She does not joke with those she calls family and her actual family. That is why I have to mention her when I talk about this part of my life. We grew up as sisters; we often wore identical clothes and were told we looked so much alike. This made us extra close. We have remained sisters despite the distance between us and have remained close.

I first opened up to her in 2018 when I was planning my fortieth birthday. She couldn't understand it at first because she only saw what

I presented to her. Once she got closer and saw a couple of things, she started to understand, but still not fully. It's hard for people to understand what I went through. In her case, she was trying to understand what I needed her to do. Who was messing with me? The problem this time was that a marriage was involved, and children were involved, so she and many were being careful. She would ask me, "Are you sure?" "Do you want me to intervene?" "Should my husband intervene?" By the time I opened up to her, it was too late. I was already beginning to detach emotionally and could not see a way forward.

When I finally told her the whole truth, she sympathized with me and told me not in so many words: "Whatever you need." She recently shared with me that she was angry about many things and I sensed she wanted her usual opportunity to fight on my behalf, but she has respected my feelings and where I am with it all thus far. She only needs to hear the words, and she will pounce.

Like I said, she loves family and is truly sad for me that I lost the structure of mine, but not my whole family. She has often expressed how proud she is of me for taking steps to protect myself and admits that she did not understand it all until recently.

It's okay because I love her and all of my family for not seeking to understand on my behalf, but just being there for me.

You need someone who does not need to hear your side of the story to know what part you played in the story. That's my cousin. She knows that if I say I am done with my marriage, then I am done. She knows that I would have done everything in my power to make it work before giving up. Her only question to me still is "What do you need?" and I know she means it.

Perspective

The people I have mentioned are those who are closest to me and have been with me throughout this journey. Many have come and gone, and many are just joining.

These are my flies. They hover around me with my stench of shame, guilt, pain, disappointment, and hurt, and they stay on the wall waiting to pounce on anyone who messes with me. They flock to me like bees when my flowers bloom and help me pick the petals when my flowers wither. These are my flies.

Who are your flies? How do they support you? Jot them down in your journal. I bet it will make you feel warm and fuzzy or make you cry or just feel less alone.

Discussion & Reflection Questions:

- Who are your flies, gang, squad, girls, boys?
- How do they support you?
- Who could you make one, if you have none?

Use the following journal pages to write out your thoughts.

Part 2

"I am so tired, tired of working and struggling...of deflated dreams... disappointments...being taken for granted...playing the game...falling for tricks...sleepless nights...tears...anxiety... sympathy...no sympathy...being angry... being sad...tired of trying.

JUST TIRED."

KEEPING UP WITH THE JONESES

My mom always told me that all fingers are not equal. When she said that I always thought, *Yeah, right. But I still want those new shoes.*

As a little girl I didn't lack anything or anything that I needed. I grew up in an upper-middle-class home. Things changed when my dad left paid employment to start his own business. Even then, things were not so bad. There were those times though when I couldn't get what I wanted. I can't tell if I was being greedy, covetous, or justifiably a little girl with needs. Girls have needs!

Throughout my adult life, I have always been conscious of trying not to keep up with the Joneses. Alas! I came to America and started making money and could afford things. Initially, it was little things—taking more chicken than I would have dreamt of as a child (we all know this is not a factor of wealth, parents just do that), or those shoes you see at Macy's that you don't need. I started making more money and thought I was grown, started getting into shopping from the U.K. My excuse was that I was tall and they didn't have long pants here, and so it went until I started hanging with different "Joneses," and I wanted what this person had or that person had. I could afford it, so I got it. Isn't that how fashion works? You see something and admire it on someone, and then you buy it.

Well, no one told me you had to be able to afford it.

Okay, let me back up just for a second. I came to the U.S. for college at the age of seventeen and had never worked. I knew nothing about credit history or budgeting. Needless to say, I learnt the hard way. Where I am from, there was budgeting but not the credit system.

So, I kept buying. I started to see the designers I had read about or seen in movies. I could buy them. Hmm! I started to buy. I love designer things, don't get me wrong, I'm not a saint. I started shopping by occasion. Every girl does it. As I grew older, I told myself I'll wear something from the many things I have in my closet, but I never do. I still go into a frenzy every time I have to go somewhere. I can blame it on where I am originally from because we are a competitive bunch. Like, really competitive.

It's not only about fashion. I also overcompensate with groceries for my home. Don't ask me why. I don't know. I never lacked food as a child, but I didn't also get everything I wanted, and that's normal. So why do I overbuy? I don't know. On a given shopping trip, I go to Sam's Club, the Tropical Store, Kroger, Walmart, and sometimes Publix. I know, crazy, right? My sister used to laugh at me when she lived with me. On Saturday mornings she would ask, "Are you off?" I would say yes as if it were a chore.

Anyway, during this COVID-19 pandemic, I have started to think about it again. I am telling myself I want to be less materialistic in the face of all that is happening. I am telling myself I will not rush out and go shopping for the next occasion...but what if I don't have a green designer purse? Argh. I need help.

I can blame my ex-husband all I want to, but there was a part of me that was not content with what I had, too, and craved more. He didn't help matters, but I will take responsibility for this one. He led me to the pond but did not force me to drink.

We would talk about investments and cars and things we could not afford yet or probably never would be able to. Yet somehow, we would move forward with decisions, knowing full well we could not afford the things. I would follow along on the promise of funds that never came.

So, yes, there was some inherent need for me to keep up with the Joneses.

Perspective

I've always wondered if it's a lack of emotional strength or an excess of confidence that makes people content. I don't know. I shared this part of my life because not being content led me to some of my troubles.

Why do we keep up with the Joneses? I don't know. It might be something from our childhood, our personality, our weaknesses, our friends, our family…it could be anything. For me, I think it just happens, and as we grow older, we really need to put things in perspective and know what's important and what differentiates us as individuals.

For me, I am having one of my aha! moments and would really like to be less materialistic. I want my Joneses to be people who serve God and are simple in everything they do, people who invest their money and save, people who help others and do meaningful things. I am certainly not there yet. Who would have thunk it? That this pandemic would still be on, or that it would take me nine months to finish the book. Lots have happened in these nine months.

I have been separated, been divorced, been almost a published author, been stronger, had a COVID test, had my kids go through online school, two have gone back to in-person school, and my kids have gone for their first sleepover at their dad's. I got a new job, therapy is going well, I'm healing, I can identify my trauma triggers… and…no! I'm not dating.

Discussion & Reflection Questions:

- Do you shop and hide it from your spouse? Have you done this in a previous relationship?
- Do you have things you couldn't wait to grow up to afford or do?
- Are you content? How do you know? What do you crave?

Use the following journal pages to write out your thoughts.

CAN COMPETITION BE HEALTHY?

Our society has made us numb to unhealthy habits that result in negative actions or emotions. One of these things is competition. Can competition be healthy? (I will share my perspective at the end of the chapter.)

I got a welfare call back from a very close friend of mine whom I consider a big sister. I shared my book idea and what inspired me to write and she started to tell her story. This journey has made me realize that we are all unique creatures with vast experiences that need to be shared to help someone somewhere.

My friend told me about her amazement at how people can be so fake or not genuine at such a young age. If you know my friend, you'll know that she loves hard and with all her heart. She is also confident and an authority on many life subjects, but most of all the Bible. She lives her life as close to the word of God as she can.

My friend told me the story of how she grew up, which I already knew, but from a different perspective. She grew up wealthy in a home full of love and laughter. Her house was the house everyone ended up at. Her mom still cooks for an army till today. I never had the honor of meeting her late father, but he must have been a great man—also very warm and welcoming—like the rest of his family.

So everyone came to their house. Cousins, relatives, and friends from far and wide wanted to spend holidays or time at their house. They were all welcomed with open arms.

All was nice and rosy. When her father passed away prematurely, her mom fought to maintain the lifestyle they were used to, but she was a woman in the early 80s. Some changes had to be made.

She shared with me that she was saddened by how such young children in their teens could be so false and negative. Don't get me wrong, it was not innocent childish teasing or childish competition, it was deep. They chided her and laughed at her for their status change after her father's death. This was when she was a freshman in college and was grieving. Suddenly, her house was no longer the coolest house on the block.

Fast forward twenty years later....

Some of these people can't wait to flaunt their accomplishments at my friend, but the irony is that in their eyes, they are getting back at the little girl who was born into fortune. My friend is accomplished in her own right and is doing very well with her beautiful family. But why the competition?

Perspective

I think competition can be healthy if it comes from a humble place. I speak for myself. I have seen my friends and family have things I wish I could have, or do things I wish I could do, but the difference for me is that if it is attainable, I try to attain it while getting guidance from the person who I admire. Oh! And don't forget to compliment them on the accomplishment. Some people might see you in a lovely dress and not compliment you, then go home and scour the internet trying to find the same dress. Just compliment them and ask where they got it.

Unhealthy competition is an issue in our society today. It breeds envy and negative situations. I often find myself being drawn down this road, and I have to catch myself and turn around. It is tough, people! But we all have to utilize our conscience.

Unhealthy competition is when you don't stop yourself and you let competition take over and be negative. When you inconvenience yourself to chase other people's dreams, when you don't give that compliment when you rush to the internet and can't find the dress, try to outdo your mentor or person you call your best friend, when you don't know why you are always angry at this person and why you pick fights with this particular person, it is not healthy.

Look at my friend. Twenty years later, people are still trying to compete with her younger self. That's pathetic! I don't think anyone is immune to unhealthy competition, but I do think we can stop ourselves and really ask why.

My friend asked God to weed her vine. Weed such people out of her life and surround her with loved ones.

The truth is that when you have a strong and bright personality, people will always compete with you. We must pray for only those who wish us well to surround us.

Discussion & Reflection Questions:

- Are you a healthy or an unhealthy competitor? Why?
- Was your home the cool home when you were young? If not, whose was? Describe the situation.
- Do you compliment people when you see them? Why or why not?

Use the following journal pages to write out your thoughts.

CHECK ON YOUR STRONG FRIEND

Today I have been struggling with what to write about, and it's not that I write daily, but recently I have been following my conversations and experiences. I wanted to write about emotional detachment earlier, then I changed my mind and thought about how angry I have been and how I haven't really enjoyed my children and don't really know myself as it has been one thing or the other. Then I read a post from my cousin about a woman who was physically abused and is now a life coach, telling women to tell their stories. And then I watched a TV show with my younger daughter.

I had a terribly busy day at work. I have always worked from home, but working from home during COVID is different. It's like we're all trying to prove how grateful we are to still be working. (Which we should be. Not complaining.) There's also the added bonus of the kids at home doing digital learning and just the non-stop action. It's been a lot. I finally crashed last week and had to take a few days off work. Today was my second day back at work, and my first day back at working out. I think Caleb, my trainer, was happy to see me.

Honestly, I'm exhausted.

Around 10 pm I was reading another post my cousin had shared, and I finally knew what I wanted to write about. I turned on my lamp, got my laptop, and here we are.

The post was by Jason Wilson, the author of the book *Cry Like a Man*. In the post, he said, "They need a break from being strong all the time."

He was referring to women.

I sent him a DM to see if he would talk to me from a man's perspective. We'll see!

Recently, I have been telling those close to me that I am tired. I had been telling my husband this for a long time. I was and I am tired. Tired to the depth of my bones and spirit.

I just want to take at least three months off work and travel. Go home to my country and visit family, eat the food I grew up on, not have to worry about bills and being responsible. I love my job, so I don't want to stop working, but I don't want to have to work.

I have a friend or a couple of friends and family who can travel for extended periods and not have to worry about their finances. I certainly don't want to be a kept woman, but dang! Can I get a break?

I came to the U.S. at the age of seventeen from a foreign country. My parents paid my college tuition initially, but I still worked for some of my upkeep. I have worked every day except for after giving birth to my children or looking for a job, which was never longer than two weeks because there was never anyone to cover me. I am now forty-two and I am still working. I thought I did everything right: went to school, did well in school, got the job with Fortune 500 companies, worked hard....

I'm not sure if I really knew what I wanted, but what I didn't know was that at the point in my life when I felt tired or wanted a sabbatical from work, I wouldn't be able to take it.

I have always been the strong one in most relationships. I don't know why. I don't want to be strong, but I cannot change who I am. I cannot pretend not to care if my mortgage is not paid or bills are not paid. I cannot turn a blind eye to my responsibilities, but I don't want to be responsible. I want someone to catch me when I fall. I want to have choices. I may sound irrational, but I want what I want and I am going to pray it into existence.

I want to have a "feature toggle" as we call it in software development. I want an on and off button. I am always on.

I am extremely hardworking, too ambitious, and always learning something. I love it! I sometimes wonder whether I'd be so driven if my life were not so hard.

I love the good life, so I am willing to work hard to have it. But I always wonder if the women who get the good life and get to take breaks from being strong have two heads or are aliens. They are just women like me. When I talk to some, they tell me how they turn blind eyes to things, or truly don't notice or get bothered by stuff. (Did I tell you I'm a worrier? I can worry for the world.) Some of them are just lucky with partners or have really found their soulmates. Some of them are so mean and end up with good men. Yeah, yeah, I know karma is a B, but you don't atone for karma. Is it a lifetime thing? Jeez! I'm tired.

Perspective

I sometimes compare this situation to the emergency room. If you're not bleeding from a gunshot wound, you wait. If you show people that you're strong, they will assume you are. I got comments from friends during my separation from my husband like this one: "You mean you were going through all that? Wow! You carried it with so much grace." Does that mean I should pass out from grace?

I am healing from many wounds, but I am the only one who can fight for myself as I alone understand.

I don't judge people who are enjoying life because they are blessed or know how to play the game, but I am still healing and trying to figure out the balance between who I am, what I want, and how to get it in this crazy world.

I don't know where I learned not to ask for help and where those who ask for help learned how to ask for help. I just know that I'm your strong friend, so check on me.

Discussion & Reflection Questions:

- Are you the one in this essay or do you have a strong friend you need to check on? Call them!
- Have you ever dreamed of taking a sabbatical from work? What's stopping you? Money? Fear? Job security? Something else?
- Do you admire men or women who know how to get what they want from their partners in a relationship or marriage without being controlling? Or do you find it unnatural?

Use the following journal pages to write out your thoughts.

INERTIA: I CAN'T MOVE

They say money is the root of all evil, and I say fear is the root of all stagnation.

Weekends were the only days I could catch up with friends from back home because of the time difference and work schedules. I had been trying to reach out to friends and family since the pandemic started. Anyway, this Saturday, I did my thing and decided to call my childhood friend to check on her and to also talk to someone who understood me. This was the first time I was going to tell Ijeoma I was writing a book. As usual I looked forward to a great conversation.

The phone rang and rang but no answer, so I went on to call my sister and chatted with her for a while and then decided to defrost some beef for stew. I love to cook, but as you know I like to do a lot of things and then complain. Cooking is not one of them, although my hand has started to hurt after my recent cooking marathons. Not complaining!

My friend called back about an hour later. She had been going through some marital issues as well. You see, this was her second marriage. I was checking on her because of the recent COVID-19 crisis and all the additional responsibilities that came with it.

The first thing she said to me was, "Girl, you didn't tell me working from home was this hard. The workday never ends." I had been working from home for years. We laughed it off and then talked about how my friend was doing. She shared her fear of losing her job during these times, a fear that most of us have, and also the fact that everyone was working at 150% capacity to prove themselves.

I asked her about her marriage and how things were, and she shared that things were still the same. Maybe even worse. She shared that she had been scared to do what she knew she had to do in her marriage because this was her second attempt at marriage, and it might look bad. She didn't really care what people thought of her on the surface, but we all care deep down. It's the fear of what people will think or say. She told me how she questions herself on her choice of partners and cries the tears that we all cry at night. "Lord," she said, "why me? Who did I offend? I'm sorry. I want to be free of these burdens and pain."

I sympathized with her, as I also had similar nights. We agreed that we didn't want to change who we were going forward and that we would pray for someone who would love us how we wanted to be loved and deserved to be loved. She recently left her husband and is thriving, but fear held her down for so long.

Children who come from broken homes don't fare well, they told me. I told them God raises children, not men. Even through my brave, angry answers, I was still tied down by an invincible weight of societal expectations.

I can picture myself twenty years ago, beating my chest proudly, saying, "I will never condone abuse of any kind in marriage or a relationship!" But I did. I condoned it both in marriage and in a relationship. I'm not sure what level of brokenness makes someone condone such things, but it happens to the best of us.

I was physically abused in a relationship before I met my husband, and I convinced myself that it was because I was being verbally abusive to my boyfriend. That's why he hit me.

When I met my husband and we were dating, I would say he was emotionally manipulative and then he graduated to emotional abuse.* Not sure if there is a difference, but I can tell you how it felt.

When you are in an abusive relationship, you seem like a fool to those around you. They wonder why you just don't leave, but they don't really see you. If they were to X-ray you, they would see all the vines,

**See Glossary on page 270 for definition.*

thorns, and roots that held you down. They would see that whichever way you turned there was a thorn ready to prick you, and if you tried to rise, there were roots holding you down. To escape you need to constantly fight your way out and make sure you do not get caught in any of the old vines you had escaped from.

When in an abusive relationship, your usually sharp mind is foggy and clouded with codependency and trauma bonds.

It is easier to stay than play the mind games. Or, Lord forbid, get beaten.

People who are in physically abusive relationships are trapped by fear. Fear of their abuser keeps them in place. This person is home with them and can harm them before help arrives. They are definitely trapped, and the abuser holds all the power. I am so scared of physical abuse because it is so volatile. Anything can happen in an instant. It is literally a matter of life and death. So many women and men have lost their lives senselessly at the hands of an abuser. I get it, I know it's hard, but we are speaking of life and death here. One misstep and it's over.

Emotional abuse! This is a silent killer. No abuse is better than the other, and I cannot even say you have more control over emotional abuse because you don't. Also, a lot of the time, emotional abuse leads to physical abuse.

Another thing that keeps people in marriages or abusive relationships is lack of finances to leave if you are dependent on the abuser. So many people cannot break free because of lack of funds, lack of a job to escape to, or lack of other adults to communicate with outside of the situation. Imagine an immigrant who knows no one except their abuser, who is fully dependent on the abuser and cannot work. Many live in this hell and cannot find a way out.

Perspective

Fear is a terrible thing, but we are all scared of something, so we better embrace it and figure out how to overcome it.

So many women and men stay in unhappy marriages or relationships, jobs, and friendships for several reasons. Most of those reasons can be boiled down to fear.

Fear of public opinion, fear of loneliness, fear of judgment, fear of not getting support, fear of financial stability (this one is tough), fear of speaking up, fear of persecution, fear of the next person, fear of wrong choices, fear of an abuser…I can go on.

I said earlier, embrace the fear, pray through it, and find a way to overcome it. We all have different clocks in our lives. Use your own clock to determine when the time is right for you to stop being scared.

Discussion & Reflection Questions:

- Have you ever experienced fear that cripples you? In an area of your life, school, work, home, sports, etc.
- Was the fear ongoing or just one incident that passed?
- If you overcame it, tell us how.

Use the following journal pages to write out your thoughts.

RED FLAGS

Only when you look back now do you realize they were red flags. At the time, you thought they were subtle behaviors that would surely change or could be changed because the other person loved you or wished to make the relationship work. Right? Surely, if someone is in it to make it work, they won't do things to jeopardize the relationship.

Early in all of our relationships, we all had some sort of voice or courage, so we were not afraid to speak up before the manipulation and strategic silencing began. Don't get me wrong, not all silencing or storming in a relationship is bad. It is normal for people in relationships to observe each other in the beginning, study their partner, and begin to figure things out. How to communicate, how to resolve conflict, and so on.

Most cultures, especially in Nigeria where I am from, still believe that women should submit to their husbands and be as malleable as possible. I am a true believer that men should lead their families and their wives should support them, but I don't agree with the wife not having a voice at all.

I went through the storming phase in my relationship prior to marriage, like many have. I was done with all the fighting and arguing, and I wanted out. This was surely not the way relationships were supposed to be. I was young and a lot of things went over my head. I didn't really HEAR what I was told, and I understood it in my own way. After dating my husband for about two years, I took an opportunity outside the U.S. and left. I wanted to make sure. I kept in contact and didn't really say I was done, but I had left. I stayed out of the country, working for one year. I didn't date because I still saw myself in a relationship.

After a year of living apart, I forgot how heated our arguments were and how bad it got. My husband came to Nigeria where I was and asked for my hand in marriage. What was the darn hurry, ladies? Jeez! I felt like you were supposed to say yes when someone asked you to marry them. I never saw a reality where someone said no. I didn't even think it was possible. How would I craft the words? Looking back now, it never crossed my mind. I was caught up. I ignored all the red flags that made me leave in the first place.

I'm sure you're wondering, *What red flags?* Let me share some of the ones I saw. First let me take the opportunity to say that infidelity was never an issue in our relationship to this date and to my knowledge. I don't want to know at this point. I don't think I will make it if I added that to my issues. For me, my No. 1 red flag was the silent treatment. My parents never did it, and I never saw it growing up. Sure, my cousins and I would give each other the "ST" as we called it, but I was never able to handle it or last that long in the ST game. I always tried to make peace.

Some people have PhDs in the silent treatment. My husband—boyfriend at the time—certainly did, but he denies it till this day. Another one was his response to my crying or emotional needs. I can cry for the whole of Texas and California put together. I am not sure why I didn't tap into this particular red flag, but he would not be moved. Are there really no men out there that will hold you and let you cry and make it their life mission not to let you cry again? I couldn't understand it, but I still went in headfirst.

Another red flag was his response to the tough questions. I tried, y'all, I did. I tried to ask the tough questions, but all I got was a gruffy, "What do you mean?" and I backed the heck up! Yes, I got intimidated and slowly got silenced. I really don't know where I lost my way. Before I go on, I want to reiterate that I am not sharing to throw shade on my ex or make you think negatively, but to open your eyes and correct what you can before you lose the love of your life.

Red flags continued. This one is tough for me because I really don't want to seem critical, but we're sharing, right? Work ethic. I'm not just talking about your partner's approach to work but just to any undertaking. I have always felt like I have no choice but to work hard at anything as an immigrant in the United States. I don't know if I'm lazy, but I operate from a different place of not having a choice. Based on this, I didn't understand or see what was right in front of me. It was not outright laziness—it was doing just enough to keep my guard down. The stories and plans were always comforting, and I felt I was part of something, but sixteen years later I'm still hustling as a woman and there hasn't been much progress on the other end. It was not just work—even with family or projects.

I always said in our arguments that my ex was not hungry enough, and he knew I would always hold the bag. I would always be there. I did tell him after fifteen years that it was not my dream as a little girl to be that person who holds the home together as a breadwinner and leader. I am willing to do my part but not be the insurance policy and the policyholder, too.

Perspective

When we're in love or want something badly like a business relationship, we ignore the red flags. We tell ourselves that things will change. We tell ourselves that our love will make the difference. We assert ourselves and stand on the love in our hearts. I used to tell myself, "Surely, he cannot see me crying and suffering and not feel anything." That he would soon leave the guest room where he had stormed off to and not go to bed angry. Until that became normal.

Friends don't let red flags become the norm. Once a red flag becomes a norm, it means that something inside you is not being heard or addressed. True love will listen to your concerns and make a concerted effort to correct those things. Speak up about the things that bother you to the one you love, and give them a chance to do something about it. Not everyone is perfect, but if they are not willing to lose you, they will come around before it's too late.

Friends, your love relationship is your closest relationship outside of God. You have to take it seriously and work at it. But don't ignore the fact that you cannot really change people. People will make reasonable adjustments and maintain consistency in those adjustments for the ones they love, but they will not change.

Don't find that out the hard way. Learn to manage your expectations.

Premarital counseling is one tool that I have heard is very helpful. A lot of what I described above is mainly around conflict resolution and communication. I did not go for premarital counseling before my marriage. I did not belong to a church, and I'm sure it wouldn't have gone down well with my fiancée at the time, but that's the only time you may have a voice that you can scream with. Scream for your life!

Discussion & Reflection Questions:

- What are some red flags you ignored in any relationship in your life?
- Do you regret ignoring the red flags or are they things you can live with? Why?
- Do you feel peopld can change? Why or why not?

Use the following journal pages to write out your thoughts.

PARACONFUSHOCKED

"Does Amanda Renee Jones, the wife of the person you're cheating with, know you're dating her husband?"

I almost fell off the bed. What? I—faithful, supportive, hardworking, religious, principled me—was accused of having an affair by my husband. It was unheard of. Maybe in my earlier days, but not after three children and a life of commitment.

At 2 am on a Wednesday morning, he said, "Do you ever talk or complain to anyone about our relationship?"

I did have my gossiping sessions with my friend and my mom, but I was sure he would never have heard it. So I said, "No. We talk about general stuff. You come up sometimes." I was lying through my teeth. Why was I lying? I was scared. Scared of what? Scared of having normal gossip sessions. Shoot, I didn't even know normal.

"Are you sure?" he said, in the unkindest way possible—almost threateningly, like he knew something I didn't. I could never have imagined what was coming next, though.

"Please," I said. "I need to sleep. I have to work in the morning." He did not have to get up in the morning, hence the full-on battle.

"You're lying," he said. "And I know you talk about me and how I am moody and don't support you. Why do you lie about our relationship to your friends? Why do you have to lie to gain favor?" Then he started to repeat the content of my phone conversations. Shock and an unexplained emotion was starting to set in. I can't explain the feeling. Something between fear and violation.

I was getting nervous, wondering how he knew exactly what I said, then moved to the slow realization that he must have overheard me. But what was worse is he not only heard me, but he heard the other party, too. (You know you have to have the whole story if you're the day-one confidant. If you're coming in halfway, then it's going to be bad.)

He continued. "I heard everything. And I heard what they responded to you."

I always knew this dude was slick, but not to me. We were on the same side…right? My anger rose at the invasion of my privacy. I fought back and denied some things, but there was no point because I was having an out-of-body experience. I was paraconfushocked.* (Yes, I made up a word from paralyzed, confused, and shocked.) I felt cold, then hot. I felt like I was going to be sick then dizzy. I moved, trance-like, from our bed to my favorite chair, but it did not give me the usual comfort. I didn't want to touch my phone for fear that it might ring. I couldn't watch TV because of the hour. I feigned using the bathroom, walked around my closet, and then went back to bed. He was waiting for me.

"But why? Explain to me," he said. "Why did you lie when I asked you?"

I was quiet. Feeling violated, confused, naked—let's call this one, vioconfunaked.* God! I thought. What does he want me to say? How can I make this go away? Why me? As if my life were not complicated and hard enough.

But I was still scared. In fact, I went into full recoil mode and believed things about my own conversations that I knew were not true. There were some wild accusations, y'all. Sometime around 5:40—or that's the last time I saw the time—I fell into some type of rest and was up at 6:30 am. I canceled my morning workout and escaped to my office. Eager to email my best friend and tell her what had happened. Surely I couldn't call her.

The next morning, he was sleeping like a baby. And nothing got resolved but sleep deprivation for me.

*See Glossary on page 270 for definition.

Mr. Jones, my dear friend who is happily married, didn't hear from me for two years. He called several times and I never returned his calls. I cut him off on the off-chance that my husband would think I was having an affair.

I spent the next eight months after that questioning every conversation I ever had. Wondering if I had indeed done something wrong. Wondering if I was going crazy. Did my mother really say those things during our conversations? Did my friend really mean it like that? Did I tell her about that day, or did he guess? How much of it was made up, and how much of it was real? I was just talking. I don't remember everything I said.

This is bizarre, right? I had done nothing wrong, but why did I feel like I had? The accusations, the invasion of privacy, the slander, the paranoia, and the brainwashing had all taken their toll on me, and I recoiled.

Something broke for me that night. My mind was working time and a half. It was already working overtime with our usual disagreements. This was new.

Some weeks after the main confrontation after our daily court hearing (with him asking me all kinds of questions, enjoying the control he had), I asked, "Are you still listening to my calls?"

"I will never put myself through that again," he said. "I have deleted everything."

On January 1st of the following year, he came to me and said he was leaving. He could not take it anymore. I was emotionally detached. We got into arguing, then he brought up something he said my mom had said on another one of his surveillance calls. My mom did say she would put our matter in prayer, but he said she said she would apply spiritual pressure. See how crazy it was? This was every conversation. Twisted to look bad.

Fifteen months later, he threatened to play my conversation to one of our mutual friends who was trying to reconcile us after so many attempts. He had to convince our friend I was wrong. He had to find something very bad. But he never showed anyone the recordings.

I went through hell and paranoia. First I did not know how I was being recorded. I called my phone company. I called Apple. I checked the whole house and my car. Nothing. I was going a little crazy. Some said let him hear everything—it will surely kill him, and that will teach him. Some said, "Did you check your clothes?"

Finally, almost two years later, I was starting to accept my fate, whatever it was. I spilled my green tea latte in my car on my way back from the gym and moved my chair. I found an iPhone recording under my seat.

Silly me took it to him and confronted him. And right in front of me, he took the phone and did a factory reset. Crap!

You would think that would do it. Nope. We argued and moved on. I changed my phone the first time, and I changed my phone and phone company and ID after our separation. Then I still got a company to check my phone and laptop. They found some stuff, but guess what? I'm still thinking he can hear because I passed my phones down twice to my children. So, both phones are still in this house.

At work, I started feeling like people were attacking me, and I started defending myself. People were shocked. I had to advise myself to take some time off work. If not, I would lose the job I loved so much and lose relationships I worked hard for. I was suffering from paranoia, anxiety, and depression—that's what the doctor said when he gave me nine weeks off work. Still, it was not easy being recently single with three children and activities. I finally broke down in December of 2019. My mom was there to hold me.

Sigh! He's not here, and I am still acting like a suspect in *Criminal Minds*. The struggle is real!

Something broke in me that day in June 2018. I lost trust in my love. I was wounded. My love died that day. I cannot describe the feeling still, and as I write now, my heart still hurts. He never apologized because he said I was lying.

Why does life suck so much? Why does it have to be so difficult? Can't we all just get along?

Perspective

I will let you come to your conclusion as to what was going on with me, but I want to assure you that I had done nothing wrong. There is a psychological definition for what was happening to me.

I soon came to realize that it was okay to talk to my mom or my friends. It was okay to have a male friendship as long as it was not physically or emotionally adulterous. And it was okay to vent and complain when your husband made you mad. It didn't mean you were leaving him or that you didn't love him.

I wish I knew this when I was going through all that pain and guilt.

Discussion & Reflection Questions:

- Have you ever felt a feeling there are no words for? What was it like? (You do not have to share the experience, just how you felt.)
- Did you make a resolution after that experience? What did you decide?
- Have you come to realize that you can love people deeply but not like them at a particular moment? What happened?

Use the following journal pages to write out your thoughts.

I NEED A SCAR

It's like carbon monoxide poisoning. You don't know what is happening until it's too late. Yes! That's what it was like in my marriage.

I couldn't put my finger on it because my husband had never laid a finger on me. Well, that's not true. He did one time before we got married, and it was a heavy handed sort of warning to never come at him with flailing hands and insults. I still cannot see the harm in it—I say that to say that it did not change my decision to move forward with marriage. I actually forgot about it until recently. Wow! Am I weak?

I tried many times to describe my emotional pain and burden to his best friend's wife, who I had become close to, but she couldn't get it. She was happily married and hadn't dealt with emotional manipulation* and abuse in her marriage. But the real reason was that my husband was telling her husband something totally different from the truth. She just couldn't understand what I was going on about. As far as she knew, I was taken care of, hadn't paid a bill in my life, and I was chilling—or that's what they were made to believe.

I would call her crying to tell her how I was tired of carrying all the responsibilities in the house, and she would shrug it off and say, "But that's not true. I told my husband you wanted him to talk to his friend about your complaints the last time. He said he didn't see the issue since your husband pays all the bills and he hears him taking care of the kids. Are you sure you're not overreacting?" I would change the subject, defeated. This happened in different forms over six years. I would call, and she would dismiss it, offering coping mechanisms.

**See Glossary on page 270 for definition.*

One time my husband's best friend actually came over for dinner alone and talked to us. My husband derailed the whole conversation with accusations that he knew would distract his friend. Again, no resolution. I was shocked and couldn't get a word in. I thought I must be dreaming. How did my cries for help become about him again? His friend left that night with the advice for my husband to pamper me and for me to be more patient. Ohhhh, he didn't like that I had invited his friend, but what was I to do? I was desperate.

When his friend left, he asked me, "What, did you think he was going to beat me?" I went to bed, resigned.

I stopped complaining to his friend's wife after that.

Things got worse, and I started talking to my mom. My mom noticed my husband's behavior when she visited from Nigeria and stayed with us. She also saw the burden on me, but I told her I was okay and made excuses that my husband was trying his best. I explained that he had many failed endeavors with his business and many half attempts at working full-time, but it would come together.

Shortly after all this, I started having health issues, like hypertension and vertigo, and I had to get a mouth guard for grinding my teeth.

Our kids were getting terribly busy with activities. Again, my husband was there but not there. I continued to carry the burden as I was solely responsible for the mental understanding and arrangement of the logistics. I complained many times, but he just let me go on with no real or dependable change. He would "help" sometimes, but it was really on me to figure out. I couldn't understand it. It started wearing on me, so I started to push back and connect with my old friends. Finally, I heard from other women that my story was not a lone story and other women had gone through and were going through this. My friends advised me, and I started to push back.

My husband did not like it at all. What happened to his submissive wife? Who would work more than forty hours a week, take care of the kids and the home, clean, cook, and still be ready for whatever? Why was she pushing back? Someone must be advising her. Someone must be teaching her. He descended on my mom and told her she had overstayed her welcome. Luckily, my mom left due to an emergency with my dad. I continued to push back, tried to force him to get a job, tried to split bills with him, and when he saw I was serious he would pay them for a while or "help" out for a while, and then when I relaxed he would fall into old patterns again. It was an endless cycle. It was exhausting.

He was always very good at convincing me to buy things we couldn't afford. I believed in him and loved him so much that I always fell for it. He would promise heaven and earth and even show me conversations on his phone, or speak loudly where I was, so I would think he was serious this time. Oh! The joy and relief I would feel. He was finally coming through for me. My man! My love. Then I would commit to the thing—a car, a house, furniture—and he might make a payment or two or none and then there was nothing.

This was our pattern. I was always left holding the bag. Sometimes he would throw some rubble in the wind to distract me, or sometimes he would play nice. After about ten years of this, I had had enough, and I started challenging him. He had a way with me and with words. I now know it's called love bombing.* He also knew how much I loved him, and he took full advantage of that. I was always ready to give him the benefit of the doubt. When I continued to push back after the tenth year, the suspicion in his mind that I was being coached grew. He decided to break the second to the last bone in my back by bugging my phone.

He would pick fights with me and ask me about conversations I had during the day. He was incredibly careful not to let people know what he was doing to me. It was maddening. After all, there were no scars. He bugged my phone for at least two years and used it to disrupt the home. He would pick fights about my private conversations, where I would be whining to my friend or my mom about him, and I would deny it vehemently. My friend once asked me what I feared, and I didn't know what I was so scared of. Who knows? It might have been instilled fear. I denied it for a long time because I couldn't imagine a universe where my calls were being bugged. So my vehemence was strong. This continued for about two years, and he never knew peace. When I found

**See Glossary on page 270 for definition.*

out, I told him he could not know peace because he went back to my calls to gauge every action.

When he overreacted and friends and family were called to intervene, he would turn the incident to his advantage. I could never compete with his embellished story of how he was a victim. I couldn't believe it! Wait! *I* was the victim, but everyone was long gone, and it was back to the grind and misery again.

It was endless. I was starting to feel dizzy with the merry-go-round. Always the same thing. Nobody could see me. Nobody understood. He was too slick for me. He was smarter than me. Nobody believed me. Nobody was helping me because they could not see it. I needed a scar. I needed him to be physically abusive. My claim of emotional abuse fell on deaf ears. No one could see my pain.

I stopped waiting for people to hear me or fix my problems. I fixed my own problem. I got the heck out of dodge.

Perspective

It's hard for me to write sometimes because I am still healing and because of my fear that my husband will not agree with my version of events. But I don't care anymore. I am not doing this for him. I am doing this for those of you out there who feel like you cannot tell your story or think you're crazy. You're not. I am now divorced, but I still stand in the shadows and observe myself. It's unreal. I can't believe the ride has ended or slowed down. I am now able to catch my breath and see.

Sometimes I still wish he had beat me or cheated on me so I can have something to hold on to or at least win in the court of public opinion. Sadly, all those years of working hard and holding down the fort did me no favors in real court. Story for another day. I have my peace, but I don't feel like I won anything.

"Emotional abuse is a losing game. Don't look to win. Look to live!"

—SE

Discussion & Reflection Questions:

- Have you consciously made changes during your relationships? How did your partner, boss, or friend take it?
- When you asked for help, did people understand?
- Have you heard of CPTSD? I found that I was looking for PTSD and could not identify a single event. Look into CPTSD and write how it's different for you.

Use the following journal pages to write out your thoughts.

SHHH...DON'T TELL ANYONE

I have always had an issue with secrets, keeping secrets, what a secret is to people, and how people just assume you should know not to say in some cases. I feel there is a difference between privacy and secrecy.

One time, I had spent the whole day with a family friend. They had given me a ride back from school. That friend was going on a trip with her mom that same night. Not a whisper was heard about it. The next day, I went for a ride with my friend again to school as I liked to, and there was no friend. My friend's sisters were there, and they just acted like nothing had happened. I just couldn't understand it. Were they keeping it from me because I had a loud mouth, or were they scared that I wished them harm? My family was not like that, or maybe they knew I just wouldn't keep the secret. This got carved in my brain, and I was learning. I never saw the big deal in secrets, except it was a *secret* secret that could cause harm to someone. Reporters don't keep secrets; why should I?

See, I had a big mouth growing up, and I constantly got in trouble with my family and close friends. But as I grew up and offended people by sharing their most trusted secrets, I realized that people kept secrets they wanted to keep, and everything was not public knowledge. I started to understand the impact of sharing those secrets with others. But what if they didn't tell me it was a secret? Couple of lost friends and paybacks, and I got it. I still don't like secrets or secrecy.

My husband was a very private and secretive person, and he had grown up very unlike me. Everything was a secret. I personally think it was a way to ensure his web of lies didn't collapse when it came to our life together. But based on the childhood experiences he shared, there were indeed people who wished him and his family ill, and he had learnt as a young child to keep secrets and keep things private. I, as I said, was not raised like that.

Here it was again, this whole what's-a-secret-and-what-shouldn't-I-tell thing that I had encountered as a child. Now, I ended up with the civilian version of a CIA agent. After sharing many stories with my husband, I started to understand, but it was so strange to me even as an adult. I also started to understand why those families so many years ago acted the way they did. It still did not make complete sense, but I understood. It must have been based on their experiences. Whatever! I'm still here and still don't like secrets.

I started to understand what I could share and what I could not share. Then there were times when I would share things about myself and my husband would get mad because somehow, my sharing my experiences affected him too. Again, it was that he didn't want my version to contradict his own version, so it was better I was quiet. He often accused me of talking too much and sharing too much. I totally backed down and became quiet because I associated it with my childhood blabbermouth reputation, but this was different. This was tough for me. I started hiding things from my parents, family, and friends. This was when I started lying and embellishing too. I started building my façade. These things turned out to be little or big things that could have brought me peace or resolution from internal conflict, but I was quiet. Just the little, "Oh, my husband does that too," or "My teenage son is very belligerent too," would have taken the pressure off, but I couldn't say a word.

I was to be quiet.

Apparently, I didn't know what to share and what not to share.

Then, after we were separated, oh my! This was a tough one. He wasn't here anymore, so why the secrets again? Oh, just so he wouldn't give you a hard time during the divorce, they said, or you never know if he is still listening to your calls. Just don't share your progress. It's bad luck. I get some of it, I guess, but not all.

Perspective

What a conundrum. This life is so complicated. I know I used to talk a lot, but then I get confused again. Was I oversharing or was I undersharing? I feel like I was undersharing when it was important to overshare because when I finally shared, no one believed me.

Know when to speak up, lest you end up being the villain in your own story.

Sometimes in manipulative situations, things you share when vulnerable can be used against you. Make sure you are trusting your heart and your secrets to those who will keep them protected.

So, yes, I understand what it means to keep a secret, but can we please get the definition of a secret? Not everything is secret!

The question is "How do you feel?" You have to do a self-check against your principles. You should also check with your accountability partners that you're not crazy and after that, stop! Stop hiding.

Do not spend your life with a muzzle on your mouth. Don't apologize for opening your eyes or mouth. Speak your truth and find your confidants.

Discussion & Reflection Questions:

- What's your take on this "secret" thing? Are you good at keeping secrets? Are you asked to protect secrets that could harm you?
- How do you cope with difficult situations? Do you feel you are telling a secret or you feel you are unburdening?
- Is your partner secretive or private?

Use the following journal pages to write out your thoughts.

SEE BLOOD TO SEE ME

I have always wondered if we need to see blood before we see each other.

Early, I referenced the emergency room comparison—about how you needed to be bleeding before you could get the immediate or necessary attention.

Sadly, that is the case with many relationships today. If your spouse or partner does not see blood, they often don't see you. A lot of us believe we are supporting and building with a partner, and that makes us strong or stronger in their eyes. This goes mainly for women who see themselves struggling and holding the fort until their man can catch up or catch a break. He may even have caught a break and still does not partner with you on household logistics. I call it "thinking with me" or "sharing a brain." It is also common with women as well, but the sad part is that experiences have shown that if the women step up and show strength, they risk owning many masculine responsibilities. When the women or men wise up to what's going on, there might be a carrot of some sort dangled to make them comfortable and continue supporting. Remember that these partners that are taken advantage of are in love and so are those taking advantage of them. Or so they call it.

Most couples start well out of pure innocence, or maybe not. They tell themselves they are building with their partners and buy into the dreams and plans. They buy into the promises and hold out hope for a better tomorrow. But as soon as they show some initiative of a hustler and get caught in that love hook, they are done for. They keep telling themselves they are on the same page, but somewhere along the line—five, ten, fifteen years later—they see the picture as clear as day. They are left holding the bag! They were building a dream all right, but it wasn't theirs because it sure didn't feel like a dream or the dream. It felt like bondage.

But how could someone you love and who professes their love hold you in bondage? How could someone you are working nights, weekends, and multiple jobs for, every pyramid scheme, not see you and want to match or outdo you? Wasn't a man supposed to support his family with what he can? Wasn't a woman supposed to make a home? Wasn't a female breadwinner supposed to have had that talk with her partner? Wasn't it supposed to be for a short while? How did it come to this?

They say the good guys get the bad girls, and the bad guys get the good girls. I really believe that's true. Life is a game, and you better be ready to play it!

My Friend Alicia

Alicia didn't see it coming that her husband, who was so devoted to his family and his mother, would not make a good father. She didn't recognize the weight on her because it was disguised in responsibilities instead of in monetary form. She didn't know that even though her husband paid all the bills, he wouldn't participate in raising her sons and daughter. She thought she chose right because he was so devoted to his siblings and mother. So why was he not paying attention to their children? He was driven, but his drive did not transfer to his only daughter. Alicia felt she might have been heavy handed early on in their relationship, but she couldn't figure out when. Was it when she asked her husband not to overreact on the wrong occasion when Hajara, their daughter, acted like a fifteen-year-old? Or was it when she thought she was being understanding and took his turn for activity runs? Alicia couldn't figure out where she had gone wrong, but she definitely was paying for something, and her husband was punishing her. She often wondered after six years into this behavior, how long he would punish her through his children. Did he not see he was missing out on their lives completely?

Alicia was very strong-willed and did not budge as she continued to do her best, but between a full-time job and raising four children during the COVID-19 pandemic and several years before that, she was exhausted. Her body finally cried for a break. Alicia found out she had become diabetic from stress eating and not exercising and was rushed to the hospital amid the COVID-19 chaos with elevated blood sugar levels. Now he saw her!

Why did it have to come to this?

My Co-Worker-Turned-Friend, Jemima

Jemima, another hardworking lady, met her guy at a party. He pursued her hard and she fell in love with him fast. Jemima was easy-going. She wanted to have the American dream where both parents worked, and maybe the wife didn't work as hard but still contributed, and her man supported her.

She did everything right. They dreamt together and got married. Had two kids and enjoyed each other. She hadn't started feeling the weight. Things were okay. There were carrots or even a whole bed of carrots from time to time. She kept going, doing what was needed. Five, ten years went by, and then she started to feel the weight. But this was her man, so she told him, "Baby, I'm feeling the weight. Can you stop with the dreams and get something solid?"

He dangled the roots for planting carrots at her this time. She kept going, thinking, *He's got me. Just a little bit more.*

Two more years went by, and that particular dream did not materialize. She cried out again, and he watered the carrot roots, and some started to bloom. She relaxed. Remember, all this time the weight of the two kids, bills, activities, etc. were weighing her down. She was lifting weights at the gym to be able to carry this weight put on her in the name of building and supporting. You might ask, what does she mean by carrots? I mean the occasional mortgage payment or two weeks of picking the kids up from their activities. This should keep her quiet and lifting more weights.

Nineteen years went by, and Jemima finally had a stroke from chronic hypertension due to stress. He finally sees her!

Jemima's older sister has always told her what she had was not love, but because her sister was not married, Jemima chucked it up to jealousy. Noelle, Jemima's older sister, took her straight to her house from the hospital and took the kids as well. She started helping her heal and get back on her feet.

Now her man wants to get a job and work hard to support his family.

If he didn't see blood, would he have woken up? Had she died, who would it have served?

Perspective

Stephan Labossiere said in his book *The Man God Has for You*, "You enable his procrastination, his lack of ambition, the unwillingness to do more in life and provide more for you because you are accepting it. It is hidden under the guise of support and 'building with him.'"

Lack of ambition and provision may not always be the case, but it is the sheer unwillingness to do for you that must not be excused.

I have used the word partner a lot here because I am not assuming everyone is married, and I am hoping not, so that they can make amends before taking that important step.

Relationships are about partnership. I don't mean in the sense of an active and silent partner. That never works. You often find that when companies become successful, they want to buy out their silent investors or partners because they don't feel those people have a vested interest, but who are we kidding? It's nice to be a silent partner and just get dividends or profit at the end of the fiscal year. True, lasting relationships cannot work like that because the scales will not be balanced.

I wish we could just have an Alexa, Cortana, or Siri tell us the scales are leaning too much to one side. I wish Alicia and Jemima did not need to end up in the hospital for their partners to really see them.

Alicia's husband tried to step up, but it was so out of character for him. He still tries and Alicia just tries to take better care of herself and turn a blind eye to her unnecessary OCD side while Jemima is no longer with her man.

Do we have to see blood to see ourselves?

Discussion & Reflection Questions:

- Are you holding a grudge? Why? Will you be okay if you're unable to see the person again?
- How many people in your life do you think you support, thinking you're building with them?
- Are you the passive partner or the active partner? Do you think that kind of partnership works outside the boardroom?

Use the following journal pages to write out your thoughts.

ROMANCE NOVELS ARE TRULY FICTION

So, I know romance novels are supposed to help build a fantasy and symbolize love stories, but they didn't tell us that there might be bad endings or that the characterization would not fit all of our lives.

My editor asked me if I was holding back, and yes, I have been holding back. I didn't want to get deep or too personal in this book because I'm putting my name on it. But if I'm not real, how can I help you, my reader?

I have always been attracted to guys who are slightly older than me. I justified this by saying that I am mature for my age and need someone equally as mature.

When I sit and think back now, a lot of my issues were actually from my immaturity and naivete. Isn't that ironic? Miss Mature is not mature. I mistook quiet shyness for maturity. I didn't in fact know what I wanted and what my boundaries were. I am finding that you must know yourself and your boundaries to recognize when another person is pushing against your boundaries. If you exist in a state of not knowing yourself, then you risk damage to your emotional and mental health, and in my case, physical health.

This was my story; I didn't know what I didn't want. I read a lot of romance novels and paid attention to the good stuff in them. I didn't pay attention to the men mistreating the women and how the women responded or vice versa. I didn't pay attention to conflict resolution or how true love sacrificed it all.

Thinking back to specifics of my relationships, I see myself behaving a lot like what I saw my mom do, and the sad part is that these guys were not my dad and I was not my mom. I did not know their dynamic. I never asserted myself or put my foot down for anything. It was like I was afraid to ask the tough questions, and these guys knew that. So, even if I asked, there was a gruff, "What do you mean?" or "Don't worry about it," and I would be terrified to rock the boat.

Perspective

Romance novels are truly fiction, yes. But they also show us how it can be when there is true love between two people. They show us when people have a disagreement and how they cannot live without each other.

I personally like feel-good movies. I love the Hallmark movie channel. I grew up on Harlequin and Mills and Boon romance novels. I love Danielle Steel, Jackie Collins, and Nora Roberts. When I moved to America, I also started reading Terry McMillan, E. Lynn Harris, and Zane. Yes, I love to read, and I love love love a happy ending. Did this contribute to my illusion? Oops!

Anyway, I did not have anyone telling me about conflict resolution, God's design for marriage, roles in the household, raising children, and just life in general. I learned the hard way. Maybe we should have gone for premarital counseling? But then again, somehow, I don't think it would have helped me. I would have made excuses or my fiancée at the time would have knocked it and told us not to go, once the counselor started digging.

Yeah, I just think we need more education about life and relationships. Do you agree? Am I the only one who feels this way?

Discussion & Reflection Questions:

- Do you depend on companionship, or can you be on your own? Does it depend? How?
- Have you now or in the past been in love? Describe it.
- Do you know yourself? Likes, dislikes, dreams, limits, values, principles, thresholds, red flags, etc.

Use the following journal pages to write out your thoughts.

SEPARATION

Why did I even get separated?

What did that mean for me?

It was unexpected.

As I went through it, I didn't even equate it to real formal separation in legal terms. I just wanted all the stress, arguing, sleepless nights, crying, tension, chest pains, anger, sadness, and anxiety to stop. I had made up my mind that I would suggest it once I gathered the courage.

It was toward the end of summer. My birthday had just passed. Oh! What a birthday it was. Just miserable. I still love birthdays like most and like to have one special day to be celebrated. That day like most days recently was another day of one unfounded argument after the other. I just wanted to get away.

I knew before that day that I wanted to get away. I planned a spa day and breakfast by myself, followed by an evening out with my cousin, who was visiting from another country. No plans to spend time with my husband that day. I reluctantly planned a dinner the next night with him. Why? I don't know. Out of fear or just being complacent, maybe. I was still doing what seemed right or normal. Pleasing others.

We ended up not going because I just thought, what the heck? We had argued the day before on my birthday, and I didn't want to do anything the next day. I called my mom crying the day after my birthday and just couldn't understand what it was all about. All the arguing and mood swings. I was also going through mood swings because I wasn't brave enough to do or say what I needed to say, and a part of me didn't articulate it in my mind. By this time, my mom and I had started praying weekly over the phone for other things, and we decided to spend the next week praying and fasting on the issue of my marriage. We fasted for three days, and on the fourth day, September 19th, I walked into the house from our local park where I found serenity.

My husband said, "This is not working out. I think we should get a divorce. I will file tomorrow."

I was not expecting this. But when you pray, you better be ready for the answer!

I didn't plead, but I did suggest we try other things before divorce, but he insisted this was the only way. (This was a bluff, as I would come to find out later. One of many. He had used the D word several times in our arguments, and even during a therapy session.) I got angry and spewed insults in my confusion but didn't beg. (Y'all know why women who fall on the floor begging, beg, right? They know what they are about to lose.) I didn't beg. I got ready and went to work. I called several people on my way to work and everyone had their opinion.

As was normal, he acted like nothing had happened that morning and said he was just upset. This was the fourth time he had used the D word and third time he would walk out on me. I vowed that day that it would be the last time. I told him I would not divorce him, but he had to move out so we could take time to work on ourselves and heal. He appealed to me, but I insisted we needed the time apart. That was the week I started living apart from my husband of almost sixteen years.

We both went through different emotions during this time. I went from being sick with anxiety and loneliness to sadness to self-doubt, to where I am now six months later, rebuilding and growing. I cannot speak for my husband, but from my point of view, he also went through a series of emotions too. I experienced his anger, insults, grief, but no remorse and no change. No consistency, no effort. After looking at the horizon for a speck of light and only saw darkness, I knew what had to be done. I prayed and asked for guidance, and all I got were signs and confirmation that I was not going to change this man. So after six months I decided to get a divorce.

Perspective

I had been thinking of separating from my husband for a while because things were just not working out. We had tried everything I could think of, but in my opinion, things were getting worse. We were both miserable. I thought it would be best to get out of each other's hair for a while. It was best, but it also revealed my worst fears. I always feared that he would not fight for our family and not only did he not fight for our family, he fought against our family. He did everything you don't do when separated and trying to win your family back.

I always thought separation was supposed to create space between each other, help you miss each other, realize you cannot live without the other person, help you try life out without them and then decide. I certainly did not expect what I got from separation. Our separation created further heartache, more burdens, more slander, and a fight for my life and my dignity. I was very disappointed.

I am sharing to let you know that if you are like me and hope that your separation will fix your issues, there might be another outcome. I hope yours works out better than mine.

Discussion & Reflection Questions:

- Have you left your marital home or thought of it? What happened and why did you return?
- Have you separated or taken a break from a relationship? Did it help? How?
- What did your partner do to push you over the edge? Did you separate and reconcile?

Use the following journal pages to write out your thoughts.

IT'S GOING TO BE ALL RIGHT

I made a new friend more than a year ago. We talk once a week about my life, my journey, and my experiences. Today, we talked about my journey and how I expressed to her when we met that something had to change. I told her about my pain, my fears, and what gave me hope, and we made a plan.

She said to me, "If you have a plan, it will make it easier for you to cope." At the time I didn't really understand that what I was feeling was a feeling of lack of control of my life. My buttons were being pushed by someone else, and a lot of my actions and responses were literally programmed and a result of coping mechanisms I had adopted.

By the time I met my friend, I wanted change. I had reached my limit for the time. I wasn't ready to leave my marriage, but I wanted some sense of sanity. She and I talked about some of my struggles, and we identified the things I could change that would give me some relief.

I put my plan in action. One of the main things was my financial burden, so I did something to lighten my burden. I learned about my thresholds—not boundaries, but thresholds—and I tried not to let anyone push me over the edge. In my humble opinion, thresholds are the places you get to when the boundaries you put in place have been disregarded. It's like the fence I reference is the boundary. Then they push me over the fence, in essence pushing me over my threshold, over my limit.

We talked about what I had control over. One thing I came to realize was that I could not change another human being. I said I realized but did not understand. Come on! When you're in love, hope is a given. As I write now, knowing I will not go back, I have .000001% of hope that my dreams of a relationship with my ex will come true, but then you ask me, "What will you do with that?"

I still have seventeen years' worth of sentiment, but no regret.

My friend stood with me and guided me through this journey. She said to me today, "You have always had the burden, and you also had hope. Now the burden is still there, but the hope is gone." This was after some clarifying news from my lawyer.

We talked about my journey of always being in limbo in my marriage, of all the false hope and disappointments. How I always held out hope that the person I loved would change…but he never did, so slowly over time I lost hope, and the loss of hope seeped into all areas and relationships in my life, affecting and impacting everything.

I saw on her face during our visits how bewildered she was at some of the things I would share with her. She told me how I have grown from a scared woman to a strong survivor of emotional abuse.

That friend is my therapist. She has helped me through a lot. My main source of strength is first and foremost God, then my family and friends.

Perspective

It wasn't always easy. I may sound very confident and sure of myself in this book, but I wasn't always this strong. I am a Philippians 4:13 woman. (I can do all things through Christ who strengthens me.)

God has been my rock and has answered all my prayers. I know I had to go through this experience to fulfill his purpose for me, but it was not easy. It was very painful and heartbreaking. My heart is on the mend, but there is a long journey ahead.

You need a support system in or out of marriage. You need professional help, and you need someone who understands what you're going through. I commit to being here for you, as much as time in a day allows.

Discussion & Reflection Questions:

- Do you plan for yourself in your relationship?
- What kind of plan do you think I'm referring to?
- Do you have hope and a burden? Describe how you would feel if you lost hope. Have you?

Use the following journal pages to write out your thoughts.

HE DIDN'T BEAT YOU... WHY ARE YOU CRYING WOLF?

As soon I hear the garage, my heart jumps in my mouth.

I'm thinking, *What's it going to be today?*

I guess they had always been abnormal, but it was okay because he loved me and he was probably having a bad day. Yes, things were that bad in the end. I saw a lot of signs throughout my sixteen years, but I rationalized them. My husband also did not make it apparent that anything abnormal was happening. Any time I was at the edge of discovery, he would do something to pull me back in. In Africa, we say the other person put something in their mouth to talk to you. Some of the things I committed to and took on were very herculean and not things I would ordinarily take on, but he would sell the idea to me to so well and promise support financially...but rarely showed up. He did show up when he wanted to or when it suited him and made him look good.

Initially, he made a lot of big gestures to tie me down. He often references a car he bought me early in our marriage. It didn't feel like my car. After that car, all other cars were his idea, but somehow I financed the nicer cars in the house. I cannot say for sure about the earlier cars, but later in our marriage I started to see the pattern. When he bought a car, he bought a conventional practical car that he always paid for outright, and I would always have the car payment on a luxury car.

The most vivid memory was of my last car. I told him I could not afford it, but I was having so much trouble with my car then. He said to me to go ahead and buy the car even though I could not afford it. He would pay toward the payments. Why did I believe him, when he had never done that in twelve years? I don't know. Same thing with our home—when it was time to pay the first mortgage, he was not in town. He asked me to pay it that month, and he would do it after that. I paid that mortgage for eight years and that car note for four years. Lots of arguments, crying, and bullying, but the promise was never kept.

For those of you wondering, my husband did not have a 9-5 job. He worked on random business ideas that never really took off or grew. He got by selling cars and doing real estate. He was able to do that because I was holding down the fort. Did I not say anything? Yes, I did. So why did I stay so long? I don't know. When you love someone, you always have hope for a better day. You believe in them. You think they will change because they love you.

My husband had a way of talking to me and convincing me that a red shoe was blue, and I believed it. I am a very accomplished woman, and I do very well for myself. I am not a weakling. In fact, some may call me a "boss bitch." But somehow, this guy had me wrapped around his little finger, his whole hand.

Many people do not understand emotional abuse. They can't see it. Emotional abuse is not like physical abuse where there are scars. I am not comparing as I cannot imagine what those who go through physical abuse feel (but once), but emotional abuse is just as bad. Emotional abuse creates invisible scars, and it chips away at you slowly until you don't recognize yourself any longer.

I am quite active. I work out two to three times a week. I eat right 70% of the time, and I try to be happy. High blood pressure is hereditary in my family, but I was taking two different pills for blood pressure at thirty-three because of the emotional abuse that was eating away at me.

When your spouse comes home, you should be happy, right? I was not. I'm not a confrontational person, but I was in this marriage. I felt like I always had to defend myself, avoiding an argument or happy that he was happy, which was only when he had the upper hand. I let him have the upper hand a lot so I could have my peace. Some days it was accusations. I was accused of outrageous things. I remember always saying, "I am not like that, and you know my mind does not work like that. How can you accuse me of that or thinking like that?"

He projected a lot of what he was putting me through on me. He accused me of abusing him. He said I was stonewalling* and gaslighting* him. He told me I needed psychiatric help because I was abusive to him. You know what I did after he left in a huff? I went to look for the meaning of those words and started thinking that maybe I was, indeed, disturbed. But I was still sane because I knew even if I were cray, it was as a result of what he had put me through. I was very shaken after that argument and scared. The first thing I thought was, *I will lose my children. He will say I am unfit.* I was terrified. I called my mom, and she calmed me down. (By this time, I was taking my private calls at the park near my house.)

You know what? Writing to you helped me again! People always ask me what was the straw that broke the camel's back. This was it! The fact that he had me believing that he was building a case to prove me unfit and that I could lose my kids. I started to realize I was deep in a major problem.

Perspective

Emotional abuse is very hard to quantify and describe. It is even more difficult to try and defend yourself to people who do not understand. It's not their fault though. They just don't get it. Everyone's situation is different, and every victim's thresholds are different. No two situations are identical.

People who are emotionally abused do not have scars or black eyes, but they are dying silently. Abuse causes stress and stress manifests in different ways, but the main ways are cancer, hypertension, diabetes, and so many other diseases.

**See Glossary on page 270 for definition.*

Please, let's be sensitive to those who are victims of abuse of any kind. There is verbal abuse, emotional abuse, sexual abuse, physical abuse, and many more. I am not ignoring other forms of abuse—I am just grateful that I only experienced one type and I was able to come out of it, if not whole at least with some part of myself.

I am no therapist, but please, let's become aware in these situations and be kind.

Instead of asking, "Why are you still there?" Ask, "How can I help?"

Discussion & Reflection Questions:

- Are you verbally, emotionally, or physically abusive to your children?
- Have you experienced abuse?
- Did you seek help for your trauma?

Use the following journal pages to write out your thoughts.

OPEN BOOK OR POCKET BOOK

Just before I started writing this chapter, I had heard statistics being thrown around that the No. 1 cause of divorces was finances or money. So I did some research, and trust, communication, transparency, and commitment are vying for the top spot. So I can still write this chapter on finance because they are all the same difference, as we say in the southern U.S.

I don't feel I have the best positive example of finances in a home, so I spoke to my inner circle, and I was amazed at what a life I had been living.

Guys and gals, please don't be afraid to talk about money as soon as you can in a serious relationship. It's important to know your partner's thoughts and behaviors regarding money. Are they transparent, closed, frugal, selfish, generous, clueless, uneducated, shy, great, a saver, bargain hunter, or money worshippers? I will use my favorite line here: "Don't be afraid to open your eyes."

Let me talk about myself a bit. So, you don't know what you don't know. I am only realizing now what I didn't know by talking to others. I didn't ask the tough questions. All through my dating life and marriage, I was always shy when the topic of money came up. I was not the one who would ask for things that I was entitled to as a girlfriend, or demand what I needed as a wife. I just didn't do it. My partner had to be a mind reader, or we should have set ground rules.

I think I am (or used to be) like that, I hope, because growing up, I never saw my mom ask my dad for money. He just knew when she needed money. What I didn't think about was that the conversation must have happened way before my time or behind closed doors. I also left home early and moved to a completely different system than my parents, so it was weird. Anyway, I messed up, and I don't want you to make the same mistake. Apparently, I am late to the game, but for those of you who don't know, you need to have the money conversation and you can still have it now. It's not too late. I will share three situations, and as always, we will talk about perspectives.

Joanne's husband Dave is a busy exec and she was a stay-at-home mom. I asked her how they did their finances, and she told me that right from the beginning, they had the conversation around how they would handle their money. Their agreement was that Dave would give her a household allowance, and they would discuss any new developments and re-evaluate their needs. Joanne is a trained accountant, but when Dave's job took them to California, they decided that she should quit her job and become a stay-at-home mom and take care of their three children.

Mind reader or not, her husband knew he would need to step up since they decided that she should not work. To date, he still gives her the household allowance. She has learned that he likes to give bulk money and trusts her to handle or disburse it as she sees fit. Joanne is frugal, and her husband is open about his money. Joanne knows her husband does not like money conversations, so she keeps them few and far between. They even discuss when he gets a bonus and what they will do with it. This sounds like music to my ears. They have an agreement. They have a system.

Look at Samantha and her husband, who come from a tribe where men are expected to be established financially (level depends on class) before they even think about marrying. I love that. Don't be trying to marry someone's daughter if you don't have your act together—we ain't trying to build with you! (Okay, maybe a little building.) So, her husband Dwayne takes care of the household expenses, and Samantha, who is a schoolteacher, uses her salary for her needs. They discussed this and determined that her salary was too small for anything else. When there are major expenses, they regroup. They like to talk often about money, unlike Joanne.

Let's talk about Christina and Connor. They combined their finances from day one. They both work and decided that was the best way. That trust was established from the get-go. Their paycheck went into the same account. (Wow! Now that's trust.) They agreed they would be open and upfront about their finances due to past relationships where the reverse was the case. They had both names on all accounts, and according to Christina, they looked at their money as a bucket. They were conscious of realigning when there were major life events that may affect their plan.

Connor said they made sure to share the same vision. Connor is a finance guy, and Christina didn't like the Dave Ramsey kind of life initially, but she started to see the benefits. They paid each other an allowance to do as they wish. Christina said it felt like they were both rowing a boat, and one person could not be going in a different direction, like she had tried to do initially. It just didn't work and made things harder. Plus, it just caused arguments. They also shared accountability on what went out and talked about it. Christina shared something that really touched me and made me realize that I might be in my 40s, but I was still a baby in many ways. She said, "We want to know where our money is going, because we want to tell it where to go." That was so powerful. I was still hiding shopping bags in my car! SMH.

Another thing I found great about Christina and Connor is that outside of money, they have a close relationship and are friends. She is not scared to tell Connor if she has spent money where she shouldn't. (I guess it also depends on your tastes.) The three couples I have mentioned also make decisions together, so there are no surprises. Everyone has a say.

Finally, financial experts suggest another option. They say couples who both work can have their money separate and have a household account. They decide what goes into that account.

Perspective

I tried not to share negative examples, and for those who have figured their finances out, I am happy for you. For those of us who are still hiding, I say this; when you are in a relationship, you need trust, honesty, consistency, accountability, friendship, empathy, and a little bit of frugality in your finances. There are probably more things, but these a just a few.

You need to trust that your partner is honest and has your back. You need honesty so you can trust and relax with that person. You need consistency to avoid disappointment, and you can believe in each other. You need accountability because you don't know it all. Friendship so you can talk to your friend when you mess up. Empathy to feel each other's pain and struggle. You need someone to be frugal so you have money to fight over. And lastly, you need communication because no one is a mind reader.

I don't favor any method as I have not tried any of them, but it is the intention behind it all that matters.

Oh, before I forget, parents: teach your children about money! How to manage it and have value for it. Let them see how hard it is to come by. If you are blessed with wealth, still teach them.

Discussion & Reflection Questions:

- Are you the big spender, or are you frugal?
- Would you consider yourself materialistic? What's your kryptonite? (Mine are pound cake, bags, and shoes.)
- What is most important to you in a partner?

Use the following journal pages to write out your thoughts.

AROUND THE DINNER TABLE

"When I visit you at your home in Atlanta, there is no warmth, no dinner table conversation or after-dinner family time like we used to have when you were young," my dad observed, after many years of visiting me—and also when I finally let him into my world of hurt.

When I was younger, we didn't have a perfect family, but it was as perfect as this little girl could get. My mom was a stay-at-home mom with a sewing business at home, and my dad worked as a biochemist in a brewery. My mom would pick us up from school and take us to the Dallas bakery to get bite-size cakes, and we would go to the upscale grocery stores UTC and Leventis. Boy! Nigeria was very post-colonial, and things were actually working well in the economy because we had to prove to our colonizers that we could do it and we were truly independent. I live for such simple times.

We had a tag system to help with reducing traffic. Each household had two cars that they drove on the odd or even number days, based on their tag or license plate. If you had one car, then I guess you took public transportation on those days. Not sure. (Tuesday and Thursday, you drove your odd-numbered car, and Mondays and Wednesdays you drove your even-numbered car. Fridays and weekends were not controlled, I think. I can't remember.) Anyway, in our house, we were fortunate to have two cars, so my dad would of course take the appropriate numbered car to work since he worked, and my mom was a stay-at-home mom.

The cut off for the restrictions was 6 pm, so my brother, my mom, and I would wait by the traffic warden or controllers post for 6 pm when you could drive any car. We would go to my grandmother's house to get something fun for dinner, or maybe a side dish, or just to see her. I really don't know. I don't even know if we went every day. It sure seemed like it! Now that I think about it, it might have been the time when my grandfather left her for someone else, and she was trying to cope (another strong woman). Yes, that was it! She was always so grouchy, and I always wondered what a miserable life she must live, but I met her at her most painful time. She wasn't always what I imagined a grandmother to be, but I could see her trying. She was very strict but gave rewards. She tried to work through her pain and not project it on others, but everything was an opportunity for a lesson. She was doing her best in her circumstance and protecting us in her own loving way from the bad world. Sadly, too late. She is gone now. She had her sweet moments, and as an adult I totally get her now.

My granny. I wish I had met her in her happier days. My mom says she was always strict, but she had a heart full of love. Even I could not see that as a young girl. (Sometimes from the end of her bamboo can, she used to threaten us.) I wish she had shared some words of wisdom that would have helped me with my marriage and relationships, but how was she to know...she gave me my dear mother, and for that I am truly grateful. Grandmothers are so special, and I wish I had the fairy-tale grandmother, but I got my own grandmother, and I am thankful. Enough about Granny. Tell me about yours? What did you learn from yours? What were some of the simple memories you have of growing up before this world became crazy? Do you often long for slower and simpler times like I do?

I always knew I would have a career. But I didn't think about how I had grown up. I didn't think about the fact that I didn't have a system on how to raise children how I wanted and be employed full-time as well as lead a family. Oh, how I hated leading my family. I absolutely abhorred it. Making decisions, pushing for prayer, pushing for educational growth, being the disciplinarian. I hated it and did not have any training on it at all because my dad had led.

All I imagined was weeknights like I had when I was younger—my mom waiting up for my dad on the days he worked late to eat dinner with him when he got home. I would hear the horn of his car at the gate and rush excitedly to the opening at the staircase, where I could watch him come in and greet my mom. Then I would watch him say, "Let me go and make sure those rascals are asleep," with a glint in his eye. I would rush to my room with my brother and cover my head with my covers and pull my toes way up, giggling. He would come to our rooms, pull our toes until they cracked, and tickle us a bit. That was the highlight of my day.

Now, I would just grunt at being woken up from any semblance of sleep. Our weekends were filled with some evenings of us dancing to Michael Jackson or my dad imitating BB King on his imaginary guitar (my dad actually played the guitar as a young man). Some Friday evenings, my dad would take my brother and I to the nearby country club for swimming lessons, where he always got me cheese balls.

Much later, my dad left paid employment to start his own business, but these are the memories I had and the plans I had for my own children. I had dreams of doing homework patiently, watching or reading National Geographic with my kids, doing special projects with them, being a fun mom, and living for my children. (I still live for them, but I do it through work.) It's something that weighs on me because I wasted a lot of time hoping that my spouse would share in these dreams. Now, I feel like I am running out of time to spend time with my babies without financial pressure and time constraints. (Who am I kidding? Our lives are a mad rush. We need to slow down.)

So how did I become this overworked, grouchy, mean, irritated, short-tempered, impatient, and regretful mother?

I feel like I failed them. I have tried my best for my babies and still try every day, but oh, how I wish I could be rich and turn back time so I could spend time with them. (But Seme, did you ever consider that you might not be that mom? Hmm.) I can dream, right? I may not be that mom, but I want to be another mom to my kids. I don't want to get mad when they ask for things they need because I'm strapped too tight. I want to spend time with them instead of the daily grind. I want something of the time I had as a little girl. I want to enjoy my children.

Perspective

This is probably the dream of many baby boomers like me. Maybe we want too much? I know we can't have what our parents had, but we have to craft something out. This cannot be the end of the story. Since becoming separated, my kids observed that I am less grouchy and more relaxed. That, I think, is a combination of wanting to ease the effect of my decision on them and the fact that I didn't wait hand and foot for hope that wouldn't come. I find comfort in the fact that I am in this alone for now and I can make a plan.

Please enjoy your children if you brought them into this world. Don't let anyone or anything stop your dreams. It may not be like you thought, but I trust you can be creative. Don't be like me. I am trying to course-correct, but the hustle is even realer. They grow up too fast. Oh, by the way, people say, "Enjoy them when they are young. They will soon go away, and you will miss them." Yet to feel that....

One day at a time, one small thing. Dates, laughing more, dinner together. Intentional dinner. Whatever you choose, let it be something simple. Not another thing to worry about. It will feel awkward at first. Eventually it will be normal and it will serve as the foundation for great memories. Try to course-correct.

At the beginning of the chapter, my dad was raising a lack of connection through a lack of gathering as a family. I didn't realize my deep longing for that connection as a family, like the family I had growing up, until writing this chapter. You helped me again, my dear readers!

Another thing I missed and my children lacked was the nurturing side of a partner and a father. My dad would close down the house at night, unfailingly, and make sure we were all in bed. Tell us stories if he could and tell us goodnight. My husband did this when I asked but not consistently. He did not see it as his role. Try to gain connection and nurture your family. Today I lock up and check on my kids. I don't want to, but I do. As I'm working with my editor on this, she says she would rather have her husband do this for her than have a million dollars. Wow! There is something about the act and the safety it makes you feel—it's almost like a blanket.

I lost myself, but now I'm coming home and working to achieve my dreams.

My oldest is two years away from going to college. Where did the time go? I think I can get back to my dream of how I want to raise my kids, but I have to hurry. I feel the weight of wanting their childhood to be like mine, but finances, time, and reality are not on my side. As women who have to deal with all those dynamics, how do we find the balance? For one, don't feel you have to do it all. You will get overwhelmed and give up.

Here's what I'm doing:

I'm being intentional about our meals together.

I'm spending time doing the things they each like with them. (Only my nine-year-old has time for me. Wow! I lost so much time. It's okay.)

I try to take them on dates for one-on-one time. Nothing extravagant. A walk in the park, ice cream, etc.

I believe I still have some time, so I will use it to bring my family around the dinner table like I always dreamt.

Discussion & Reflection Questions:

- What are some childhood memories you would like to or already share with your family or children?
- Have you created new ones? Share them.
- Do you wish you could turn the hands of the clock back? What would you do?

Use the following journal pages to write out your thoughts.

MARRY YOUR FRIEND

Today is April 11, 2020 in the thick of COVID-19. What a mess! An eye opener.

My plan today was to wake up early and rush to Walmart and get toilet paper and a few things. Come home, pray (like weekend prayer, not the lazy weak weekday prayer, ya'll know what I mean) and binge watch *Ozark*. But a close friend who knows my story called me this morning and said she had a story to tell me.

She wanted to talk about herself, which was refreshing, and I was honored she trusted me.

She like many of us also has her struggles in her marriage. She did not marry her true love. She told me how she struck up a conversation with an ex-boyfriend and how they were so similar and had become so successful. She shared the intellectual meeting of the minds they had in their conversation and how she felt that he got her. She missed having someone push her and encourage her, someone to catch her when she fell and someone to criticize from a place of love. She realized she just wanted to be a woman and take care of womanly things, but that was not the case. As good as the conversations with this ex were, she knew they had to stop, but he helped her strategize at work and advised her on a level she had never enjoyed.

After a few weeks she tried to cut it off, but oh, how she craved the emotional escape. It went on for a just a week more, and then she cut it off because choices had been made long ago, and we have to live with our choices. Plus, she said to me, too many people would get hurt, and who was she kidding? She wasn't about to leave her marriage for someone she knew so long ago.

These conversations really made her realize that she did not marry her friend. Why? She said she thought about when the kids grow up and it would just be her and her spouse left alone. She realized that over the years when left alone for a substantial amount of time they argue because they have nothing in common. She went on to talk about family trips and how they always ended up so miserable, again nothing in common, and of course this isolation period is testing so many marriages.

Why did she stay? Many reasons, but from my perspective pure fear of public opinion, fear of what it would do to her children, fear of loneliness, and so many other reasons. I stayed for my kids, fear of public opinion, fear of being vulnerable with the next person, fear of loving again, fear that my spouse would be with someone else and do all the things he didn't do for me. That he would blow up. LMBO. What crazy reasons. What are yours?

On the other hand, I spoke to my cousin earlier this afternoon and she told me about a bad break up before her marriage and how she felt she was lost without her ex and how she would not date again. But then sometime around Christmas of 2013, she decided to get over it and even date casually like guys, and in the process, she met her future husband. But she didn't even know it at first.

She prayed for God to send her a friend that would let her be herself and who she could allow to be himself as well. She also wanted some of her father's characteristics. (My uncle is a sweetheart, but maybe she didn't want all his characteristics because of the time in which he grew up. Not sure.) She asked to be able to recognize him when she came across him, and although not at first, she did recognize him. Today like many couples I am sure they have their struggles, but we talked about how they both know each other's boundaries.

My cousin is a lawyer but now a stay-at-home mom, but she and her husband still can't wait to tell each other things and get each other's opinions. Her husband is a successful executive who travels. How is she coping with the isolation? She says it's wonderful that he does not have to rush off the phone or to a meeting and she does not have to do so many errands. They are enjoying each other.

I, like so many out there, must say I fall into the first category. Although I don't have an old flame calling me, I too feel like I didn't marry my friend. I thought I was fine and doing okay, but I realized over time that I had nothing in common with my spouse. It's funny, my friend mentioned family trips—they were interesting. You know when you try to convince yourself that you're having fun because you've already paid for it and taken the time off. I mean...what do you do? You force yourself to have a good time. It was always interesting because my husband always wanted to explore and look for certain types of food and I just wanted to rest. I didn't mind the occasional dinner and outing, but I'm a room service, stay on your patio, get a massage, and nap kind of vacationer.

Perspective

My friend who texted me this morning: is she a bad person? Is it her fault or her husband's fault that they cannot have good conversation? No one is wrong. It's just the way it is.

My cousin: she was lucky, blessed, and strong to possess the ability to articulate her thoughts and experiences early. She was also lucky to have her painful experiences early. Experiences touch us in different ways. It is the ability to take what we will from them to move on. That is the rub.

I personally feel I am immature in being able to quickly put things together in my mind and really understand what it means without getting all emotional or placing blame. I am learning though and I am writing this book to help others see this.

Marry your friend! Don't marry someone you want to fix or who wants to fix you. Don't settle, don't be scared that you'll be the last spinster or bachelor. It sounds beautiful to be able to be yourself in a relationship. I have not experienced it, but I look forward to it. I am by myself and enjoying doing what I want. (Maybe sometimes I'm a bit much, but who cares—life is for the living.)

Discussion & Reflection Questions:

- Who will catch you when you fall?
- Are you and your spouse/partner intellectual equals? If no, how does he/she make you feel? How do you make him or her feel?
- Are you constantly trying to fix your spouse/partner, or are they trying to fix you?

Use the following journal pages to write out your thoughts.

DECISION TO DIVORCE

After waiting for a change and countless incidents proving there was no change, I did what I knew I should have done a long time ago.

The most painful part is that the separation did not yield any changes. I set myself up for that one, didn't I? What was I expecting? Why would I feel like a separation would yield changes?

In my experience, I have only seen people coming back together and one partner accepting a reduced form of what they said they wouldn't, and that's okay if it works for them. I didn't do that. I just went ahead and realized that I was in a relationship that was not loving and would not work for the time being. I made the choice to move forward with divorce. Secretly, separation and divorce were to force a change in behavior from the other party which was premature and ingenuine.

I am scared, as I write, of being lonely, of not being married, of making a mistake. What if he or she changes? What if he becomes the dream person I wanted and fought to have? What if he remarries and becomes all those things for someone else? Truth is that they were not that for me. You cannot really change a grown person, or let me say, I haven't seen it happen. They may adjust their behavior and be more accommodating, but there is never really change. It all depends on the reasons you were at odds in the first place too. I am not saying it's impossible, but I am saying it was impossible in my case.

Since this recent stage in my life, I have learned that I also had some growing up and self-loving to do as well. If you are not whole emotionally and spiritually, you cannot give of yourself and love another the way they need to be loved.

I was not taken seriously during the marriage or the separation, but when I filed for divorce, I started to hear, "It takes something serious to make people wake up." "Sometimes you have to push someone for them to see you are serious." Friends and family of my spouse said, "We hear you now, what do you want?" "How can we make this go away?" "Put this on hold while we work on the issues."

I had reached out to many of them for at least six years. I went through therapy alone, with my partner, several phone conversations with my family and friends, many approaches, and words of advice. A year before my filing for divorce, a therapist told us, "I have told you all that I cannot help you if you cannot meet each other halfway and show that you are willing to work on this." The lady really tried hard through several sessions, but I feel that my spouse avoided her getting to the core of our issues. I say all this to say that I tried and put in the work to make things better. As always, I prayed and fasted before making my decision and call me crazy, but I got a sign from somewhere. It was another errant text from my spouse filled with insults.

I asked myself, "Can you live with this person again if they became an angel and met all your demands?" The answer was no. I cannot trust them. I made my decision and called my lawyers to change my separation agreement paperwork to a divorce. It was surprisingly calming. Don't get me wrong; as time went on, I had all kinds of thoughts and fears and still do, but the cons outweigh the pros. I feel sad that a union that I imagined will outlive many things was coming to an end in my mind. I have cried, but now it's just the dull ache of regret, self-recognition, and my contribution to it all that remains in my heart. Lord, help me heal.

My spouse for lack of a better word is very private to a fault. (One of our main issues. "Don't tell anyone our business." "They will thrive on your misfortune." "They will look down on you.") As far as I know, he did not tell any of our friends or his friends we were separated until I filed for divorce.

Oh, the calls and texts messages after that! Well-meaning friends and family members...but imagine, this was my day 2,920 (365 x 8) of recognizing our marriage was in trouble, and this was their day one. Welcome to the party, but I'm leaving! I was not ready to relive any pain for anyone. I was about me and me alone now. It was time to stop trying to please everyone. My wise friend says, "We always want people around us to be okay with everything we do." Ain't that the truth.

He did ask me what he could do so we could get back together. I told him nothing, and that's the truth.

Perspective

Nobody goes into marriage expecting a divorce, but life happens. I feel that my fellow Africans and strong Christians make it hard for people around them to leave a marriage that is not working for them. You hear things like "Divorce is too final" and "the Lord does not want divorce." Those are human interpretations.

I respect the sanctity of marriage, but if it isn't working and you have done all you can, please, leave. If you are in an abusive relationship (any type of abuse), please, leave.

The labeling and side eyes you will get are not more important than your well-being.

Discussion & Reflection Questions:

- Are you contemplating divorce? Do you believe in divorce?
- What are some of your pros and cons guiding your decision?
- If you don't believe in divorce and you want to get out, what will you do?

Use the following journal pages to write out your thoughts.

VICTIM, NOT VICTIM

So I was supposed to call this chapter "Flying Monkey." I couldn't. I would be talking about our friends and family. Who even comes up with these names? I fail to see the concept of a monkey flying in what I want to share with you or what Google describes this as. Anyway, let's see. You tell me if you see a monkey flying or the analogy of one.

The position of friends and family when a marriage breaks up is very difficult and confusing. The poor things don't know what to do. It was even more complex in my case because I had enabled the façade for so long. It was hard to believe. How would I take apart this perfect structure I had built? I was the builder; my husband was the architect. It had taken us nineteen years to build. (We were together for nineteen years, married for sixteen years, and still married in the seventeenth year as I write. Courts and corona! This is for my mathematician readers. I know y'all are checking.)

Around the tenth year of marriage, my fears that things were not normal or okay for me started to bubble to the surface. We hadn't had it easy, but I was in for the long haul. I held hope and stood firm as a pillar of support. Around this time, the paint around my drywall or plastering started to peel on my pillar. I started to speak up to my partner. In year twelve, the actual structure of my pillar started to crack.

I reached out to mutual friends to intervene on my behalf. "How?" they said. "What do you mean you are having trouble in your marriage? You guys are perfect. Your husband provides for you and your family, he takes good care of you and provides a roof over your head." I admitted to certain things, but I was scared to divulge all of our secrets as to what happened within our walls. (I wasn't ready.) My husband brought up some stuff about my mom and derailed the conversation. This did not give our friends a chance to help. We left the situation unresolved and went back home, each feeling what we were feeling. I was discouraged and puzzled. I'm sure he thought, *Great, I dodged a bullet.* He did ask me in a later argument what I had gained by talking to our friends.

From that day, I was changed because I saw how it was to be, and I started realizing something was seriously wrong but I forged on. In year thirteen, we continued our dysfunctional façade. The cracks were getting deeper. By year fourteen, I reached out to a close friend's wife and my personal friend. They comforted me and asked me to try different things, which I had tried. They couldn't understand where all this was coming from. I finally convinced the wife of a mutual friend (the ones I had talked in year twelve) to talk to her husband to intervene again. He did, but my husband told him a totally different story from what I was saying. So it was hard for him to choose. He's a guy and he is his friend.

Later, in year fourteen, we had the whole phone-bugging debacle and I reached out again. They still did not believe it because he still wouldn't admit anything.

Now I was no longer the victim—he was. Why was I being difficult? Why was I running a smear campaign against him? Why was I rocking the boat? Why after all this time? It couldn't be true. No! they said. You're being too emotional and sensitive. But he does all this stuff for you, you are ungrateful. When I said I was done, they said stay. You have been okay all these years, why leave now, just manage, turn a blind eye to some things, take a walk or a drive when you're upset. All marriages are like that.

In year fifteen, we were separated. This is when the flying monkey syndrome really started. Friends and family came to me and asked what happened. (It was and is the first question out of everyone's mouth, because I was a master builder), not you and him, we look up to you, you're so quiet, you're so happy.

People appealed to me. Don't make any rash decisions, think of your children, give it time (eighteen years was not enough), give him time, you take time (how was I supposed to take time with three children, a full-time job, and the responsibilities of America and Africa on my shoulders), he's just upset, you're just upset, oh, oh, oh, and my favorite—what did you do to make him listen to your calls? He wouldn't just do that.

All this time he was telling them a different story or keeping up the façade, and here I was saying something totally different after eighteen years. Surely, I was crazy and going through a midlife crisis, they thought. She's just an unsatisfied woman after money. If he gets himself together, she will be fine. By the way, there were many more people involved at this time. All our friends tried to do the right thing, which was appealing to me. Husbands sided with him, and wives agreed with me but still had to be loyal to their husbands. I became a bone of contention in the homes of the brave women.

I got many calls telling me to change my mind, many calls asking me what happened (he had told them nothing), and I had to relive the whole thing over again. I was in a state of constant defense. Defending myself and trying to convince people that I was the victim and not him, but I had built that house too well. The exterior was beautiful and perfect, but the interior was cracking and would one day shatter with me inside it.

Perspective

Do I blame our mutual friends for believing what I asked them to believe for so long, and then turn around several years later and say it was all a lie? No, I don't. Do I blame his friends and family for taking his side and trying to persuade me to see his reason? (Whatever it was.) No. Do I blame the guys for playing male solidarity? No. (By this time, most of the guys I knew were his friends. It didn't matter to me.) I know that the truth will come out one day, and if it does not, I don't care.

My friends and my family who really know me well understood that for me to take the stand I did, something must be seriously wrong.

They know how much I loved my ex-husband and my family. They knew I was in for the long haul. They knew me, and that's all that mattered. Friends will be put in difficult situations and be forced to choose. God will surround you with those people who are yours.

I had my support system, but it was still hard to have people I once was so fond of tell me to jump into a burning building and pretend I wasn't roasting. It's a journey. You will go from defensive to I just don't give a flying fig!

Discussion & Reflection Questions:

- Do you have flying monkeys around you?
- Do you often have to defend yourself to others in your relationship?
- Did you lose friends in the divorce or separation? Were they originally yours or your spouse's friends? How did that make you feel?

Use the following journal pages to write out your thoughts.

Part 3

"I am stronger today
than I have ever been.
I am free."

UNDERDOG

They say in order to heal you have to find the trauma that caused you to be an empath or caused you to attract the kind of love you do. Through this journey of healing, I have started picking memories.

I mentioned coming from a large extended family. I am starting to remember bits and pieces of my childhood that I had blocked for obvious reasons.

Do you feel that people are made to feel like underdogs, or they just feel like that?

When I think of childhood trauma, I immediately think of my parents and then I get nothing. So, I just think, well, maybe I'm just unlucky in love. I have seen therapists, but I have not seen anyone who was able to pull traumatic memories I had blocked. But congratulations, readers! You challenge me again. In order to try and help solve our conundrum of being empaths or attracting people with narcissistic traits, I had to dig deep. I'll try to visit a therapist who specializes in this and get back to you before the end of this book or in my next one.

I was talking to my friend, and we started talking about how we are empaths and how our personality makes us operate in a certain way. We are both people pleasers. We started to think back, and she couldn't find anything significant, but I found some things.

As a child, I was adored by my parents and had many variations of nicknames from Angel. Angelo, Angelico, Angeme. My uncle still calls me Angelico, and my dad called me Angelo in his speech on my fortieth birthday. I am a daddy's girl but also very close to my mom.

Also, as a child I was compared a lot to my other cousins of the same age a lot. So and so was prettier than me, so and so could take a joke. I had an aunt tell me constantly that I was not ladylike, and I was not pretty. (Inside joke: everyone said I looked like her. Go figure!) My cousin, who was one of her favorites at the time, would say we should go visit her and spend the weekend since she was single, younger than our parents (her brothers), and cool.

I would protest, "She's going to pick on me, she's too mean, she doesn't like me, she likes you." My cousin would say, "Of course she likes you. She's your aunt. You take things too seriously—she was only joking." I'd go with her reluctantly, and my aunt would not disappoint.

I had another cousin who was older and would compare me to her sister, who was my age. She had just come from the U.S. at the time and it was a big deal. She had lots of candy and cool stuff. She and her sister also knew lots of games like Red Rover and Capture the Flag. We would play on teams and everyone would pick teams, and I would be one of the last to be picked.

There was always someone richer (we were middle- to upper-middle-class and didn't lack) than my family growing up who knowingly or unknowingly rubbed it in my face. There was always something. There were many more occurrences, but these are the memories I could pull out without professional help. I know some of you are thinking that kids can be mean. Well, boohoo! It affected me, I think, or at least played a part. I will tell you how one day. When I know.

Oh! Then I came to the U.S. at seventeen after living a very sheltered life. By this time everyone was grown, my cousins were tolerable or I avoided the ones I didn't like, I avoided my aunt like the plague, and I knew I was beautiful and tall but still a people pleaser.

When I came here, I had to squat with my cousin who lived at her parents' house but was a stepchild or not the child of the current wife. Sigh. Not this again.

My dad paid for me to be on campus, but I had to spend long holidays and long weekends at their house. It wasn't pretty. It was hard for me to squat with anyone or even understand the dynamics of polygamy when I had never been exposed to it and never lived outside my parents' home.

I went about life naive, pleasing people, trying not to be a snob (so I dated some characters I had no business with) and just generally was clueless. I was clueless as to what I wanted. Clueless as to what I didn't. Clueless as to what a clue was! Just going through life trusting and dumb. My wise friend says it might have been better if I had attended some college back home to get some street sense.

Hence, my question at the beginning: can people make you feel like an underdog, or do you just feel like that? Did my experiences and all the one ups make me feel like an underdog? Yes. Did people make me feel like one? Yes, and it stuck. It definitely affected me, but I can't put my finger on it. More to come....

Perspective

I am happy with myself and have few regrets about my upbringing and my life. I have no regrets about leaving my marriage, but I think my hunger for acceptance got me in trouble there. I wish I had spoken up more as a child, but what's a girl to do? What do you really say? I love all my crazy cousins and call them out often on this stuff, but it is what it is.

Most of all, I am grateful for each experience and the strength and grace to dig deep.

Don't go through life as an underdog. There will always be someone or something better than you or what you have. I have learned to be content, confident, and am working on healing.

I believe I will find love again one day and that I will be in a better place.

Discussion & Reflection Questions:

- Are you ready to dig deep and do the work needed to heal?
- How will you do this work? Therapy, small group, coach, family, etc.
- Does this essay bring back any memories or make any connection for you? Talk about it in your journal. Use it to help identify tools to build better relationships.

Use the following journal pages to write out your thoughts.

FENCES

Many people are fortunate enough to know what type of fences they want around their home or hearts.

I wonder if people are consciously building those fences and know how to keep them maintained, painted, reinforced, and looking good. I don't know the answer. What I do know is that I am forty-two years old, and I am just learning what boundaries are from my therapist, who referred me to the book *Boundaries* by Drs. Henry Cloud and John Townsend.

My therapist asked me if I knew what I wanted and didn't want in my next relationship. I told her, "Hold up, lady! I'm still married and just separated." She was testing me. At the end of the session I realized I didn't know the meaning of boundaries. So, she asked me to read this book. The book is amazing! It is a bit long, but it is worth getting into. Even if you don't finish like me, you'll get a lot out of it.

The Oxford Dictionary defines boundaries as "a line that marks the limit of an area," and *roadtogrowthcounseling.com* defines relationship boundaries as a process of determining what behavior you will accept from others and what you will not. Yeah, yeah, this is all good and well, but how do we set these limits?

If we wanted to build a fence, we would simply mark out the area we want to fence and have documents to prove it was our property and build the fence. Whenever anyone trespasses, we would invoke the law. It's a bit trickier with emotions and relationships. The lines are not cut and dry. Things are not black and white. With people and relationships, there is a lot of gray space. Relationships are intangible. Being a natural empath complicates things even further. It is hard for me not to become emotionally intertwined. If I am not careful, I can twist myself up so tightly that I am suffocating.

I mentioned I didn't know what boundaries were, and so I didn't really create boundaries for myself in my family life. I mentioned earlier how I would do things and grumble. In *Boundaries*, the authors state that "an internal No nullifies an External Yes." Wow! That's me all day, errrrrday! I have always felt the pressure of offending people around me, and so I would agree to things but not really want to do them.

In my close relationships, I did not set boundaries and never really objected to many things that went against my values because of the fear of offending my loved ones. This has happened to me time and time again. I also used to get angry at my close family when they asserted their boundaries, but at the time, I didn't realize what they were doing.

No wonder it was a surprise to my husband when I started exercising and communicating my boundaries. He must have been in shock. I feel for him now, understanding what he must have been going through. But even when you assert your boundaries, those who love you should either get more intimate with you and appreciate you for sharing or they might get offended and you know where you stand.

I wasn't so lucky. I totally confused the poor guy. Where was the compliant and dutiful wife he had come to know the last fifteen years? Don't get me wrong: I wasn't a total pushover. But I would give in with the slightest hint of a disagreement, or just to keep having a good week or day.

Why am I sharing this?

I want you to know that I am still learning the meaning of boundaries so I can learn how to create them in my relationship, so I can avoid resentment. I can't unlearn a lifetime of doing things a certain way in a year or two. It takes time to unpack the old luggage—look at everything and decide what to keep and what to no longer carry. I am taking my time. Examining everything. This time it matters too much to rush through. I am being intentional and deliberate. I am repacking my luggage with only good and life-giving things.

I have an update for you. I was recently able to identify a relationship that had clear boundary issues, and I am working on creating boundaries, but if I can't I'm out. One thing to recognize is that relationships are not do or die. Marriages, romantic relationships, and some other types of relationships can be tough to break away from, but if you exert your boundaries and they are not respected, tell them peace out, homey!

My therapist pointed out to me in a recent session how commendable it was that I recognized the boundary issue earlier. Yes, I'm not a pro yet.

Try it out and see how it feels. Put it in your journal.

When you do what you don't want to, the Bible says we are lying or staying in a place of compliance. Can you relate to that? How does this sit with you as you start to assert boundaries?

My writing has led me to explore some things about my childhood. Throughout this process I have refused to look at my childhood for many of my reasons for not being equipped to deal with life because again, I don't want to offend and even more, feel like I am betraying my parents or family.

My family was very close, and I was very talkative as a child. They called me parrot, pocket lawyer, and so many related names. I started to reduce my assertiveness. I started to shrink a little bit on the inside. I started pulling away from others a bit and from my true self. I was too much for most people, so I started trying to become smaller and smaller.

I'll give you an example. Remember how I wanted to be a lawyer? I really wanted to be in a courtroom, fighting out, but I think I started gearing toward corporate law for the fear that I talked too much. Hmm…it's all making sense. (Scared me is trying not to seem like I am blaming my parents, and I'm not. They couldn't have known.)

Then there's my extended family. We are also very close. There were a lot of us, and we would go to my grandparents' house in the country for summer. Everything was a fight or quarrel: food, bath time, who would go out with my grandparents…we just fought. During these fights, remember I told you my big brother is a lover not a fighter? My cousins were quite assertive—it comes with our temperament from our part of the country. We are like New Yorkers, but the gene missed me somehow.

I was always crying or hurt or offended, and they would always make fun of me. "You're too sensitive, cry baby, nobody likes a cry baby, can't you take a joke?" This made me stop sharing my feelings, so I resorted to being quiet and agreeable to fit in or I would tell someone close. I've always known what I wanted. I stopped being who I truly am because I never wanted to rock the boat or make others feel uncomfortable.

I think you all (readers) just helped me figure out some childhood trauma. Whew!

Thanks, ya'll.

Perspective

This chapter may seem incomplete and it is so by design. I am still learning the meaning of boundaries and what mine are. I am healing from years of compliance and always wanting to please everyone and so I cannot jump to creating boundaries. I am taking baby steps. Maybe you are too, and that's okay. One thing at a time. Rome wasn't built in a day.

I got into this mess turned blessing because I never wanted to rock the boat, but the boat capsized. Get it?

In trying to protect my feelings and avoid awkward situations, I created an even bigger mess. It's like when someone says they are coming to visit, and you don't ask them when they are leaving before they get there. Once they get there, it gets awkward to ask because it seems like you don't want them there. So awkward!

Has that happened to you? Maybe not everyone is like me, but I bet you have some stories. Jot them in your journal, have fun laughing over how far you have come or how far you have to go. Let's do this together. We can call the next book *Building Fences* and we can put in all your stories! Fun.

So! I say this all to say…build your fences, and don't be afraid to share your boundaries. We must teach people how to take care of us and love us.

If not, we are doing them and ourselves an injustice.

Discussion & Reflection Questions:

- Do you know what your trauma triggers are?
- Do you understand what some of your boundaries or no-nos are?
- Practice your newfound boundaries with an easygoing person.

Use the following journal pages to write out your thoughts.

LAMENTATIONS

I feel like I am waiting for the other shoe to drop, literally.

I don't feel angry. At least not as angry as those who love me are. Maybe I am spent and have no anger left. Nah…I think I'm still confused as to what exactly happened to me. Can you imagine that?

I'm here alone with my kids, lost the love of my life as I know it today (hoping to have another one day), and I'm just going on. I wasn't given much choice in making my decision, but I was put in the position where I had to make a one. I tried everything: crying, wailing, begging, brave-facing, therapy, threats, separation, and ultimately divorce.

I finally made a choice. I said, "No more."

My therapist has a questionnaire in her office, and it asks a series of questions, one of them being if I had any suicidal thoughts since the last meeting. Some days I say no and some days I tell her I want to talk about it. Y'all better not call DFACs (Department of Family and Children's Services) on me. I'm not suicidal. I would answer her question by saying that some days I wish God would just take me and save me from the misery that was my life. I also told her that some days I thought I would fall down and die from all the responsibilities and the business that was my life. Some days I told her I felt like my heart would stop from my blood pumping so hard from stress and high blood pressure, which was a condition I had come to have. So no, I'm not suicidal, but the thought of death often crossed my mind, then I would remember my daughter's graduations, or weddings or my son's college basketball years at Duke where he wants to go. Who would push them, who would guide them, who would love them like me? And so, I kept soldering on.

I didn't and don't want to be a soldier. I want to be a woman to do my part and be taken care of. I want to work at my job but not worry about money because I have worked so hard.

I want my man to love me and cherish me, I want him to take care of me and say to me, "I see you're tired today, let me take care of dinner," or even better, "Your job is too demanding, let's make a schedule for the kids so I can do more." I want my man to pay the bills (I hate the act of paying bills, so I only pay them during the day or at the weekends, never at night close to bedtime). I want to talk to my man about my day and have him understand not because he knows my line of work but because he knows me and loves me. I want him to make me feel as if it's us against the world.

I am so tired, tired of working and struggling, tired of deflated dreams, tired of disappointments when I did everything right, tired of being taken for granted, tired of playing the game of have the right answer, tired of falling for tricks, tired of running around helplessly, tired of sleepless nights, tired of tears, tired of anxiety, tired of working out and looking good only to be treated like I am a sack of potatoes, tired of no one understanding, tired of caring if anyone understands, tired of advice, tired of sympathy or no sympathy, tired of being angry, tired of being sad, tired of seeing others progress (I know it sounds bad, but I have worked hard), tired of not having enough love for my kids, tired of being unhappy, tired of being deceived, tired of wondering if I am crazy, tired of caring, tired of loving and not being loved back, tired of giving the benefit of the doubt, tired of trying. Just tired.

I used to ask the Lord, "Why me?" Why did I have to try so hard, why wasn't I prepared for life or the game of life? Why wasn't I more assertive? Why was my life so difficult? Why didn't my husband see me? Why didn't he love me like I loved him? Why was I going through this pain? Was there something I was atoning for? Did I offend someone who had cursed me? Why was I never able to break even? Why was I always struggling? Why, why, why me?

Perspective

I see why now. God was preparing me for life after these so-called troubles. I was being prepared for greatness and to be able to help others in my situation.

I am still on my journey, but I don't ask "why me" anymore. I am focused on how my life experiences and story can help others. I am bound and determined to use my experiences, good and not so good, to help other women find their purpose and their path.

Writing about my experiences has jump-started my healing process and is giving me strength.

Discussion & Reflection Questions:

- What's your lamentation? Write it all down.
- Do you have a journal in which you write your thoughts or daily tasks down?
- What can you do to make the task you dread the most less of a chore? (For me, that task is paying the bills.)

Use the following journal pages to write out your thoughts.

HOLDING BACK

I started working with an editor/writing coach. Writing coach, is that even real? Yes, it is. I have always been one to respect people's gifts and professions because I know I cannot be a nurse or a teacher. I give them much respect, but as I experience life more, I am starting to see that just in general everyone cannot do everything exceptionally to skill/money making level. My writing coach is one of such experiences. She knows how to help me bring out what I want to say. Wow! She's good and she listens, she validates my pain, and encourages me to express myself. Like my dad told me, she also says, "Write! We will clean it up later."

Why am I talking about cleaning it up? I am talking about that because of my fear. What do I mean? You see I don't want to feel like a victim even though I am one.

After my writing coach read my scribbles for the first time, she said she thought it was good, but that I was holding back...and I was!

I was scared that people would read it and it had my name on it. Wait, what? Isn't the book supposed to be read? There's my crazy mind playing tricks on me again.

I have been having trouble putting down my experiences as they relate to emotional and narcissistic abuse because I don't want to seem negative and mainly because I still don't believe it happened to me or it was intentional.

The truth I am coming to find out is that whether it was intentional or not does not matter because it still happened, and I was on the receiving end of it.

My writing coach asked me to imagine it happening to someone close to me or my sister. It was still difficult for me because I kept trying to figure out if it was intentional or not. Was it all planned? What part of the treatment was intentional and what part of it was unintentional and sheer habit? It goes back to the question earlier about if your partner is unwilling or unable.

My spouse and I have been separated for almost a year now, but I cannot tell my story without feeling like I am betraying him. It is MY story and my pain. I am the victim, but I still feel obligated to protect him. Whether intentional or not, abuse is abuse, and it disrupts the victim's ability to think logically and be brave.

I still love my spouse very much, even though I know he hurt me a lot. (There it is again, that thought that it was not intentional, but it happened. It was real.) Some have said, "Why should you even care what he thinks? He's not even here." But my mind has been wired a certain way. It took sixteen years of wiring. Ten months is not going to rewire it.

The power of your abuser is real. Y'all! One day during our separation, my love, my heart, the person I would do anything for, the person who was supposedly asking for my forgiveness, asked me something and I said no. And he spent the next ten hours texting me insults. He didn't care for my emotional state because he was hurt, and that's all that mattered. He accused me of unspeakable things and insulted me for ten hours, y'all.

At first, I responded, but after a while I stopped. Even in my responses, I was still telling myself that I was not being angry or insulative because I didn't want to implicate myself. Really? I would always be polite and matter of fact. I'm not sure if I had it in me to outright curse someone out or if I had argued with him for so long to no avail, but I just didn't rise to the bait. I had been living like this for so long and telling myself, "It will be okay soon. He's trying."

One day I realized that it doesn't have to be so difficult. I had to remind myself that I didn't ask for much, so I could get the strength to stand by what I knew was my truth. That truth was that I was being seriously taken advantage of and being abused by the person who vowed to love and honor me. (There it is again. Darn it!) The struggle is real, y'all. This is me. I have walked away from an abusive relationship, but as I type, I still don't believe or understand what the heck happened. How do I heal if I don't really know what happened?

I'll give you an example of what I mean by I don't know what the heck happened, how this thing messes with your mind. My spouse bugged my phone for a long period of time. Some say it was two years, and I think it was less because I didn't want to believe it. He picked fights with me based on my private conversations he had overheard. When confronted, I denied it up and down out of fear of rocking the boat or his wrath. He might ghost me forever this time. Who knows what scares me, a grown woman of forty-two?

Anyway, in the early hours of the morning one day in June of 2018, I guess he couldn't take it anymore—he confessed to listening to my calls. Fear gripped me. I started trying to play back all my denials and conversations. It drove crazy and made me very scared. Why, you ask? I don't know. My friend said she thought I was in danger when I emailed her (yes email, this was some CIA ish) to tell her that I would be staying away for some time to think about my life. I was terrified. I cut off from a lot of people at that time. The things that scared me were: 1) what he might have heard (I was talking smack about him because he was stressing me out), even though they were my private gossiping sessions, and 2) how he had listened to my calls. To this day I don't know. This kills me because I am just starting to have peace and think I don't give a flip what he hears, but sometimes I still wonder. Last year I got a flip phone and used phone cards to communicate in 2019. I also got very paranoid, wondering if the listening device was in my car, or my house, or my car keys. It was crazy, y'all. I consider myself pretty fearless, but this guy had me scared out of my mind.

Perspective

If your abuser does not truly change or show remorse, which will not happen in 99% of cases, you lack closure and it's hard to heal when you can't really put your finger on what you're working with. I still feel like he is listening to my calls even though I have sold the house, car, and changed keys.

I feel exposed.

I hired a forensic investigation company to check my devices. I changed phone services and phones out of paranoia. And yes, I still don't see myself as a victim because I tell myself maybe I should not have been talking about my husband to my friend or anyone. He would have changed, right?

Folks! The truth is that no one has the right to invade your privacy like that. It messes with your mind and it takes a long time to recover. (Still don't know how long.)

Identifying yourself as a victim in abusive situations is very hard because of the manipulation at play making you believe that you're being irrational or overreacting. Plus, when an abuser knows you're figuring them out, they will find another button to push. They are master button pushers.

So, you ask me if I'm holding back? I tell you yes, it sounds like I'm holding back. I am a victim, but for my sanity I refuse to believe I'm a victim.

Discussion & Reflection Questions:

- What are you holding back?
- Now, like Meredith said, imagine your pain is happening to someone you love and want to protect. Now tell your story!
- What did you find?

Use the following journal pages to write out your thoughts.

CRINGE

I'm sure you have all been wondering how I fared in the bedroom through all of this.

I did okay by my standards, but my standards were not enough.

When will we start to understand that the human body is all connected? Your brain cannot be in overdrive, your emotions in disarray, and then you're horny. Even if you are, it definitely won't be toward the object of your predicament.

I was talking to a close friend today, and she asked me why I hadn't talked about the role of sex and its emotional connection in marriage or serious relationships. I told her I didn't think it was appropriate, but she said to me that many people are experiencing a breakdown in their marriages, and the loss of a connection in the bedroom was one of the first signs of trouble.

In my case, I was always very attracted to my husband, but it was truly more of an association with the fact that he was my husband that sealed the deal between my brain, heart, and body. I would tell myself that he was my husband, and this is what I was supposed to do even when we started to have trouble. I felt mute to refuse him even though all I wanted was to turn away from him and say no. But I didn't say no. In fact I only said no twice in my marriage. Many other times I just prayed he was not in the mood. (But which guy is not in the mood for sex?)

What was my fear, you ask? I was scared he would find sex outside of our marriage and that was something I didn't want to have to deal with in addition to all our other problems. When our issues became really bad just before our separation, I sometimes wished he would go and find sex elsewhere, but the possessive jealousy kept me wanting him. I also feared my mind telling me I was not being a dutiful wife. Oh, how I wish I could shut my obedient, compliant mind up. Where did my mind get off telling me what my responsibility was? My mind wasn't around when all these so-called rules were put in place. Oh well.

The refusal and disconnect started in my brain and transferred to my body. I started to cringe at his touch. He noticed and made comments like he felt he was with a stranger and that I didn't love him anymore. I didn't confirm or deny. I still could not bring myself to admit it.

While talking to my friend, we also talked about the reverse where the men are actually emotionally and then sexually distant. I am not an expert at this, but from what I have gathered, some men become distant when they are dealing with something difficult that affects their emotions, and since men are not naturally vulnerable like women, they bottle it up and it affects their sex drive. Then they become sexually distant. Then you get the "nothing is wrong" answers. Some see their partners as the enemy because they are closest to them and can pick up on their changes. Some take it further and look for solace in the arms of another. Some resort to pornography, and some just share their pain with their partners.

All in all, this leads to a breakdown in the marriage or relationship. Women start to cringe, and men withdraw. The truth is that this type of disconnect causes the other partner to question themselves. Am I not pretty enough? Am I not manly enough? Is it because I am broke? Have I gained too much weight? Is it someone else? The list goes on. Communication is key no matter what it reveals.

Perspective

Sex certainly seems to be one of the top terms of a marriage/relationship agreement. It is like there is nothing else. All roads lead to sex.

This is true and so we must deal with it and not compromise it. I don't know if what I did was the right thing, probably not, because I didn't let my husband know that our issues were affecting us in the bedroom. He should have known. It's common sense. My pastor once said to the guys in church on Father's Day, "Don't spend the whole day watching football or soccer and not serving your family, only to come to your wife at night when she is exhausted and ask for sex." Not cute.

Men withdraw or act out when they are mentally stressed out as well or if they are no longer attracted to their spouses for whatever reason. My take on the whole marriage and sex thing is that we need to speak up and seek help before it gets too bad in the bedroom, or else there will be no marriage. Sex is important—I am not sure how it became the most important thing, but it is—and it makes or breaks a marriage. Please don't keep your partner guessing. Don't pretend and certainly don't cringe like me. Seek help, talk about it, and don't let the disconnect build.

Discussion & Reflection Questions:

- Are your issues creeping into your bed?
- What are you going to do about it?
- Do you feel obligated to have sex even if you're angry with your spouse/partner?

Use the following journal pages to write out your thoughts.

DOORMAT

I watched this video today of two guys talking on a radio show. They were talking about a person being a doormat and finally having enough. The analogy one of them used was so apt. I couldn't have thought of it. He said to imagine a dog lying in the corner. Every day you pass the dog, and it is quietly sleeping or watching you. You do this for years, and then one day you're walking by and the dog jumps up and bites you.

That's the story of the doormat. That is my story and why my husband and everyone around me thought I was crazy. I never stood my ground, and then one day I decided to, and it was like a crazy rabid dog had been let loose.

I went with the flow a lot of times because I don't like confrontation and sometimes things just seemed too little to make a big deal of, but the things added up. It was like by keeping quiet, I never really spoke up about what I wanted. I felt I did a lot of times, but the conflict and arguments that ensued discouraged me from doing it often or following through and sticking to my guns. I agreed to so many things I didn't want to, all in the name of hope and love. I never saw the long-term effect it would have on my life or my marriage. I am still a sucker for giving in, but only with people who truly love me.

Hmmm...can someone truly love you and make you do what you don't want to do?

Well...did you tell them what you don't want? After sixteen years, they should know, right? So, this brings me back to our earlier puzzle. Was he unwilling or unable? I think unwilling here.

What are some ways for empaths to communicate their feelings and boundaries? We don't! That's the issue. Let's try to open up to this a bit. Baby steps.

Now that I think about it, I only called this chapter "Doormat" so I could use the analogy above. I was a doormat, but I wasn't always the dog lying in the corner. I tried but I wasn't strong enough, aware of the game or willing to sweat the small stuff. I am very sure of what I want, but I know now that love is a different game. I was in love and trusted that it was what we wanted and what was best for us.

Ohhh, we. That is such a trigger for me now. So many marriages have been broken by "we." It's we when you're the pawn and me after the game is lost.

"We." I feel like that should be a chapter on its own.

Anyway, back to the doormat. I was participating in a movie I didn't get the script for. I was playing a game I didn't have the rules to. Maybe nobody did. Maybe it was an episode of *Survivor* or *The Amazing Race*, and I thought I was the camera man, but I was actually in the race.

Perspective

The guys on the radio show said we should speak up sooner. Give signs of our dislike and confront the issues. What if you're like me? You are so trusting, and you just don't see it until it's too late? What if when you see it and decide to stand your ground your spouse, partner, friend, or co-worker thinks you've gone mad? What if like in my case, your spouse wants the quiet little maiden he married to replace the woman I had become? What if they reject your defiance?

I'll tell you what I did. I stayed on it. I kept speaking up, kept fighting back. Kept teaching this man how to love the woman I had become, kept trying to let him see my love was still the same, but life had added wisdom to me that would benefit us, kept being strong, kept bracing for the silent treatment that would follow, kept finding other ways to deal with his rejection, kept binge watching shows until I was sleepy to avoid arguments. But! I said my piece. It was sixteen years late, but I said it.

The hope is that this person loves, values, or respects you enough to understand and fight for you, whoever you may be but come what may, doormats wear and tear.

Discussion & Reflection Questions:

- Did you snap like me, or what happened?
- Was your defiance received well?
- Were you always defiant and maybe need to find another way?

Use the following journal pages to write out your thoughts.

FINALLY ANGRY

So, I have to whine.

Why can't we get blood work back within hours or minutes? Where are my scientists? Please, work on it pronto.

Let me tell you! My mind was spinning, y'all. Every thought was running through my mind. I told my friend and sister that I was sure I had the strain of COVID that hadn't been discovered yet.

Oh, what happened? I was feeling weak and couldn't keep my energy up for nothing. I bought green juice, got a bunch of vitamins, and did everything I could but couldn't get my energy. I was weak.

I was sure it was the emotional roller coaster I had been on these past months that was causing my weakness. It had finally caught up with me, but I still went to the doctor last to be sure.

As I lay in my bed thinking I had COVID, I thought of my children: what would they do? Would they be okay? I thought their father's vindictiveness was directed at me, and even if he took it out on the kids, it wouldn't last. After all, they were his blood. When I was making my decision to separate and divorce, I remember thinking, "I did most of it, so I can continue to do it, shouldn't be a problem."

It is catching up with me, peeps. I had some hope that somewhere along the lines, the vindictive behavior will stop, but I don't think he's being vindictive, I think he just does not see past himself. I mean, how do you explain not being excited about milestones in your children's lives. I can! He said to me, "If I was here, I wouldn't miss all this, and I could help you out with activities. Remember I used to take them for their activities." What he is really saying is I will miss out on my kids' life to punish you and punish them, and I will watch you suffer because I have no empathy.

I am now angry!

I wasn't angry before, but I can now be angry because I know it's not about me. I am angry because I did everything I could. I am angry because I worked late. I had hope...I carried heavy burdens for you. I know everyone thinks their kids are awesome. My kids are awesome. I am angry that anyone can let anything come between their love for them. I am angry because you claimed you were "helping" me with the kids. People, nobody is helping anybody. Both parents are responsible for their children. Angry because you played the same game you played with me, with our children. You only gave me empty promises, high hopes, last minute disappointments, and piecemeal emotional availability.

I am angry because you let my babies down. Most of all, you let God down. Children are a gift from God, and it is our duty as parents to cherish the gift. It is a responsibility and an opportunity we must not fail at.

I am angry because you deceived me into thinking you were a family man, but you were running circles around me all along. I am angry that you led me on for so long, I am angry that I am now broken, need to heal, and sometimes don't know where to start, I am angry that I find myself here at forty-two starting over, I am angry that you wasted my time, I am angry that I cannot stay in bed and lick my wounds. I am angry that I have to wake up every day and put on a brave face for our children. I am angry that there was no wisdom or benefit gained from marrying an older man, I am angry that you took me from my family with the promise to cherish and honor me and did not, I am angry that I trusted you with my heart and my life and you smashed my heart into pieces and I almost lost my life. I am angry for so many other things, but my heart hurts, so I'll stop.

However, I am not angry that because of your disappointments I learned to have a plan B. I am not angry because I am an even harder worker because I have no one to depend on. I am not angry because I learned what I don't want if I get in another relationship. I am not angry because I am closer to God now. I actually pray for myself, not our issues anymore. I am not angry because "I can do all things through Christ who strengthens me" Philippians 4:13. He has given me so much strength and courage and shows me every day that I will be okay. So, no, I am not angry—but I am!

Oh, by the way, my iron was low. I was not weak from all this anger I have been carrying around, in case you were worried about me.

I wish I had known that sooner.

Perspective

Earlier on in this book I talked about not feeling angry because I wasn't sure what was happening. Well, it took me to be sick in bed with nobody but me to still get up and show up for my kids to realize why I should be angry as heck.

I do take it as an experience, but I must admit it was a long lesson to learn. I know, I waited too long, but if you think that, you have never been an empath in love. I have learned what I needed to learn, I am healing, and I am committing to help other women not get to the stage I did.

I'm still angry y'all made me write this. Or maybe it's my writing coach, whom I love to love. (Mere, is this relatable enough for you?)

Discussion & Reflection Questions:

- Are you angry?
- Write another page for anger in your journal.
- Then write a page for gratitude. I will do the same.

Use the following journal pages to write out your thoughts.

MUFFLED TRUTH

Today I was complaining to my therapist about my weekend.

I was telling her how I had sent my book to a few people for endorsements and the feedback I had received. (This chapter is an add-on.) I'm a scaredy cat and people pleaser, so the feedback got to me, but I prayed about it over the weekend and talked to several friends about it. Can you guess which group of people had the most problems with one of my chapters? My Nigerian friends. Surprising that my family (also Nigerian) thought it was my story and I should tell it how I wanted to. A few friends said it was my story too, but some did not say that. The people who told me to be careful not to seem bitter and that I should have waited are mostly people who have gone through similar struggles in life. I found it interesting, but I did take their feedback into account during prayer. I concluded that I would still tell my story, but I had to agree with one of them to take the sting out of it.

How many times have you been told "Don't tell anyone" or "You can't say that"? I have heard this so many times from so many different people. Some mean well because they are protecting you and preventing you from getting jumped. Others are protecting themselves. In my humble opinion, being told not to tell can be very stifling. If we don't tell, then how will things get revealed? How could societies have evolved to this point if the pioneers didn't tell?

I really thought I could write my story in peace with no cultural weights muffling my truth, but I was mistaken. Who was I kidding? This book will be published and people from all walks of life will read it and come to their own conclusions. My hope is that it will help those it is intended to help.

I often say this is not a call to leave your marriage like I did, but a call to thrive in your current situation, make it work, identify yourself in your own life, and become alive!

My African culture calls for concealment of pain, pretense that all is well, and muffled truths. Women and men are gagged with cloth ties so as not to speak their truth. My question is if we don't speak, how do we move from point A to B?

The Bible says, "My people are destroyed for lack of knowledge" in Hosea 4:6.

For many years I hid behind the guise that I was protecting my family and myself, but all I was doing was preventing myself from getting help or confirmation of what a normal life should be like.

I have heard of countless people who have remained silent and their lives or stories consumed them to the point of no return. Many people are scared to share their feelings because of what they have been told. Some have been told that you don't share family secrets, or it is bad luck to talk about this or that. Some convince their partners that their situation is better than the next person's or that most homes or relationships operate the same as their toxic relationship. People live in ignorance of the hell they are in because they fail to speak up. There are some that speak up to the wrong people and are hushed or exploited. There are some that speak up to the right people and get help. It is for those fortunate situations where you will speak to the right person that I write.

I have been muffled by many over the years and when I finally decided to write the next chapter in this book I was muffled again. Preventing people from speaking up comes from many intentions. I have experienced many but most recently it was not to tell my truth, not to tell it so truthfully and raw for fear of repercussions, not to tell it as blatantly for fear of offending some, and not to tell it all for the fear that I will turn away readers and come off as a bitter, angry black woman who is hurt and still hurting. I have news for you: I am, and I want to write now! I want to share with you that if and when you make a decision, I would have shared with you the hard truths. It will not be pretty or easy. I want you to know that I will tell you how I am doing when I get to the other side, but I do not want to appear perfect to you because I would have deceived you.

So, for those of you who shy away from the truth, prevent others from telling their truth, encourage others to tell their truth, advise others how to tell their truth. Here is my truth in this book!

PERSPECTIVE

People are perishing for lack of knowledge. If we don't speak up, how will we help others and help ourselves? How will we give others strength? Some of you may think I have overshared in this book, and that's fine, but I am a very quiet person usually, so this is me speaking up.

I am tired of my sisters and brothers losing the fight because they were quiet. I am tired of hearing sad stories or happy stories that could have been. I am tired of hearing family members say they didn't know. Please don't get me wrong—it can be dicey. I know if I had involved my dad earlier, it may have gone one of two ways. Go figure! So, I know it can be hard, but maybe not your dad...maybe a friend or someone. Just share your burden.

I am also glad I sought help, reached out, and spoke up to get out of a relationship that just wasn't working for me.

Discussion & Reflection Questions:

- Do you feel like your truth is muffled?
- Have you ever betrayed someone's confidence thinking you were helping them? Why? How?
- What is stopping you from speaking up?

Use the following journal pages to write out your thoughts.

DEAR JOHN

Usually these Dear John letters or any letters start with pleasantries. Come to think of it, they never taught us how to write a sad or confrontational letter in school.

Were you taught?

Well here goes...

Dear John,

I'm not fine, and I still care if you are fine. I refuse to become hateful and inhumane like I rightly should be. To this day, you hold a part of my heart and my brain and keep them in your favorite position of limbo. You exert absent control of not confirming or denying, ensuring I don't gain consciousness of how I should really feel. Well, I have news. I am taking back my power, and I will feel how I am supposed to feel for a forty-two-year-old woman raising three children alone with an absentee father. Yes! That's what you are. You are even worse because you were actually physically present but emotionally and mentally absent. That in itself is the epitome of the confusion I constantly felt.

I selflessly gave of myself for ten years without any hesitation, and then I got tired and I asked my partner for help. I asked about all the promises we had made each other, I asked when the leads were coming through, when the plans would materialize, when I could rest. But there were more promises and love bombing when I got agitated.

After seventeen years, I had had enough. I checked my heart and made sure I had done everything in my power to salvage the union before God, not man, and I was sure I had.

I still sit here writing and refuse to believe that you were intentional in your role in our family. A role of inconsistency and indifference. A role that didn't let you lead the family or heed my cries for help. A role that made me the head of the family and allowed you to refrain from true commitment. A role that allowed you to threaten to leave and actually leave your family due to no physical, emotional, or financial ties. I sit here and refuse to believe it even though it is staring me in the face. I refuse to believe that instead of seeking counsel during our separation and getting accountability partners, you surrounded yourself with "yes men" and fed them lies, turning them into flying monkeys that harassed me in my time of need.

I fail to understand how your pride and ego lost you, your family that you claimed to love, and how you feel about yourself now after all is said and done. I am waiting to see if you will one day tell our friends the truth about the real life we lived and why we are where we are. I fail to comprehend if I know the real you and who that person is. When you started to plot against your family and what your desired result was to be, I know for me it was a serious illness or death. I told you as much in my letter to you in 2014. I was overworked and tired of holding it all together while you did as you pleased and denied me help because everyone thought I was living the best life. Well, I take the blame for winning best actor in your façade.

The slap in the face is that today, you are living on your own and taking care of yourself. Paying those same bills that you refused to pay when we were together. (You will say you paid it sometimes, or at this or that time. But could I depend on you?) The sting hurts that you will pay more for a car than you would your three children in a month. That you do not bother how your family (oh, my bad—I'm out of your family now), your children have fared for over a year. I don't blame you. You trained me well, and I am here where I need to be, doing what you trained me to do. Handle things. I will do what I need to do, and I will rise. My Father above has got me.

How are you paying your bills? Why couldn't you take care of me like you promised my dad? What about the three lives we brought into this world? Ask around. What you're doing is not fathering. What happened to the bad times and bad luck and jealous people that prevented you from providing for me when we were together? They disappeared? So now you can take care of your kids. Like really take care of them, not as an option or after I catch a heart attack.

I don't even know why I still care, but I need to know. What was the plan? Somebody was going to die. Was it me? My blood pressure was off the charts at forty. I exercised and ate right, but I was heavy with burdens.

You saw it but you didn't move!

You saw my pain. Or did you see my pain? You continually tightened my financial chains and oiled them with promises.

What was the damn plan?

You fed me pipe dreams but didn't flush the pipes. What was your plan? None of us had age on our side, so I'm not sure why I even fell for some of the lies. (Oh, my heart says love. Shut up, heart!)

It was seventeen years, and I could go on, but I just want to know: what was your plan?

Yours sincerely,

The Girl You Can Hurt No More

Discussion & Reflection Questions:

- Write a Dear John or Jane Letter. It does not have to be like mine.
- Did it help?
- Now write a letter, thanking someone. (You can mail or email this one!)

Use the following journal pages to write out your thoughts.

RESIDUAL PAIN

I know I sound like a Badass Boss Babe.

I am!

I am also still someone's little girl, and I still need so much love.

I made moves and did the thing and I'm writing this book and helping women and being strong for my son and daughters and working full-time and encouraging friends and starting serious conversations. But I am still on the mend. Yes, I am. My heart was broken into a million pieces, but it wasn't smashed all at once; it was gently chipped at and bandages were put on it to hold it together. So, I could keep going. It hurt but I saw no blood, so I forged on until the bandages could not hold my heart in place anymore. I saw the sculptor and let Him in to do His work.

You know what's funny? I was paying my ex in kindness, in time, in love, in so many ways, and he wasn't even doing a good job.

It hurts, y'all, it really hurts. The wound is so big that the doctors can't sew it back together in one day. Why should they? It took so long to make. It will take long to heal. I have seen all kinds of doctors because the wound started in my heart, but it has affected my whole body in all kinds of physical manifestations. It's bad, y'all, but I'm on the mend. I removed the band aids although it hurts to see how much damage we are talking about. I can see it clearly now and I can fix it, slowly but surely.

That's me and my pain.

Then there's pain through my children. Recently, I listened to them revel about how much fun they had with their dad during a weekend away. All they did and where they went. I told them I was so happy they were getting to spend time with their dad, but secretly I was seething. I felt some kind of way.

I was happy that my kids were happy and that he was trying, but I was feeling like I was the problem all along.

It started on the Friday when I dropped them off at our meeting point (my children live with me and will start to spend every other weekend with their dad). I feel horrible, like the mother who left her marriage and made her children carry bags from car to car at meeting points and spend every other weekend with one parent. I felt like a bad mother. Then I came home and had my first quiet time alone in a very long time, and I was fine.

Then they came back and started telling stories of all they did, and I started to feel like the problem again. Was I the reason their dad wasn't committed to them when we were together? Did I prevent him from caring for his children and giving them structure? Then they continued the stories, and I picked a few things that put my mind at ease. I may have played my part in the position my children are in, but the part I played was the part a responsible parent should play. It was still hard though and is still hard. It will be hard the next time they tell me the things their dad is doing and how he is living. And I will always wonder why he couldn't do it for me.

Perspective

You are going to feel pain. You will hurt, no doubt about it. I hurt every day. I miss someone who did not treat me right and I know I will not back track, but I still hurt because there are emotions there.

I say, "I have sentiments but no regrets."

It's okay to feel the pain, but remember why you are in the position you are in. I find that there is no right or wrong in divorce, separation, or partnership; there is just what works for you within reason. I say within reason, because I don't want abusive people to misconstrue my words.

I reached my threshold, and I gave up trying to change the unchangeable in my situation. Assess your situation and give it a good effort, a good try, a good fight. Check every corner of your heart, and if it is not for you then let it go, but I always say to my friends that "true love will know your limits."

The pain has phases, and I am moving through them.

It hurts less today because I am writing to you.

Thank you.

Discussion & Reflection Questions:

- Do you feel like you're the problem in your situation? Why?
- Are you divorced/separated with kids? How do you feel when they leave to the other parents?
- Do you feel you are doing what's best for you?

Use the following journal pages to write out your thoughts.

THROUGH THE EAR PLUGS

I tried to search for the sound of a heartbeat in words.

Google said lub dub lub dub...and another one was bah-dum bah-dum bah-dum. You get the point. Maybe you can come up with something more accurate.

I started blocking my ears with earplugs at night for several reasons. My husband snored, so I started blocking my ears because of snoring. My husband used his phone and made noise at night and because I am a light sleeper, I had to plug my ears.

It is the bah-dum bah-dum bah-dum in my ears that wakes me up in the morning now. It is my alarm clock. When I was in the thick of my despair, it used to wake me up at night, and I wouldn't be able to go back to sleep, but I got meds. Now it wakes me up mostly in the morning, and I still cannot get up or don't get up, but I'm awake.

The thoughts start to flood in. Okay, let me clarify the order of my thoughts. When I made the decision to separate and then divorce, I did it because I was doing everything on my own and felt single anyway, but there is something to be said for another adult in the house, no matter how involved or not.

So, the thoughts that go through my mind in the morning. Hmm. I should pray. Did I transfer the money for the extra bills and kids' activities from savings? (I was left with a lot of responsibility and bills.) More thoughts on how I will pay for this book cover. I need to start my Facebook paid membership, but I'm scared because my divorce settlement has not been signed. I shouldn't be too aggressive or outspoken in case he gets angry and does not sign. What's taking so long, anyway? We agreed to the terms almost a month ago.

More thoughts—my eyes are not open yet, bah-dum is in the background, mouth guard is in from grinding from stress—I have to tell my branding coach I cannot do the Facebook interview until the papers are signed. I have a meeting in thirty minutes, am I ready for the meeting? I have to drop off the broken laptop at Best Buy. What does a school supply list look like for digital learning? I really wish I could finish the room in the basement, so they can have a classroom. How am I going to keep up with digital learning, writing a book, building Facebook, and my full-time job? Oh dang! My co-worker, who is trying to help me with my new project, moved our meeting thirty minutes up. (Now my eyes fly open, I take off my ear plugs, bah-dum is not as loud, and I have to get up.)

This is how I wake up every day and have been for almost two years. Just different variations. I am grateful that now it only happens in the morning thanks to meds and the Calm App.

I constantly wonder if this will always be the story of my morning.

I certainly hope not. I long for the day I will have a partner or be rich enough for a personal assistant. (I don't want to depend on another human being, but partnership is different, I hope. Haven't personally experienced it.) Yes, back to it. A partner who will plan with me and tell me it's going to be okay and actually make it okay. Actions speak louder than words. So true!

For now, it's bah-dum bah-dum . . . .

Perspective

I am confident that this will not be the end of my story or my mornings, but bliss can't come soon enough. I'm tired. I am a strong, confident woman, but even strong women or men need to rest, need respite, need love, need partnership, need collaboration, need hope, need dreams, need fairytales, and most of all need wins!

I am also sure this heartbeat is not going to be good long term, so I am really hoping for some balance. It is getting better though. On the days when I don't have much to do or if I'm off work, it is not so bad. (To my boss, it's not my job causing me stress. I love my job!)

I cannot hide that my source of strength is the Almighty God, and He constantly sends me little and big blessings that make me know it's going to be all right. Find your source of strength and have a grateful heart.

What if we make the *New York Times* Best Seller list? What if I get to meet you all one day? I want to hear about your bah dums....

Until we meet, keep your heart healthy and protect it.

Discussion & Reflection Questions:

- Are you strong and need to rest?
- What would you do with three months of paid vacation?
- Do you suffer from anxiety or have any mental health issues? It's not something to be ashamed of. Get help.

Use the following journal pages to write out your thoughts.

ICE COLD TO THE POINT OF NUMBNESS

My kids have been bothering me for years to get them a dog, and I have refused.

The mothers out there can relate. I have three kids that are in fact children. Messy, don't do their chores, play mob silence when they get in trouble. So how can I get them a dog? That's kid No. 4, as far as I'm concerned. Okay, some background, because if you know my kids, they will tell you, "But Mom had a dog when she was a child." True, but I grew up in different circumstances. Our dogs were guard dogs—they stayed outside in a dog kennel with a long runway. We had domestic staff to take care of them.

Animals and plants and nature in general are cohabitants on the earth with us. The earth is gift from the most high God for us to inhabit and one day leave and pass away. Remember your science and the cycle of the food chain? That's what it should be. No more, no less.

Back to my children: I am not used to dogs in the house. I didn't grow up like that, and I don't do things halfway most of the time. I see the responsibility of having a dog as something very serious, and I know I cannot meet that commitment, so they should go to homes where the decision is the whole family's decision.

Now let's talk about numbness. I was watching the series *Station 19* with my younger daughter (yeah, that's my baby, and frankly the one who has time for me). It's a show about firefighters. They were talking about getting numb to death as they do their jobs over and over again.

I found that interesting and felt pain for them. A firefighter was arguing with his boss, trying to make him own up to his mistake. The exact quote was this: "Surviving is what's expected of us. What kind of man did life make you?" I found it interesting that that popped up last night.

I also called my dad this morning after praying. (Yeah, I really pray on weekends. Getting there.) I love my parents' opinions and their disparity on issues. Today I wanted to hear from my dad. I talked to him about how I was feeling about this pandemic and how the TV show and some other material had made me realize how numb we had become to the gifts that have been bestowed upon us.

So! I don't know about you, but my parents usually go overboard with sharing videos on WhatsApp for days, but it's on a different level during this lockdown. My dad reminded me of some videos he had sent sometime. How elephants were coming out on the streets in Thailand, monkeys in India venturing out, penguins in Argentina, and also one picture I actually looked at where a bear was outside a window checking on pests (humans) to see what happened.

Do you not find it strange that this pandemic does not affect animals? They feel free because the human beings that usually disturb them are on lockdown. It's quite interesting! Please, please, please, I didn't say we should let lions roam free or even bears, but it is just amazing. I will let the animal scientists figure that one out.

Speaking of science, it reminded me again of the food web or food chain where each living organism has its purpose. Human beings are the most privileged of our species, but we must not become cold or numb.

Perspective

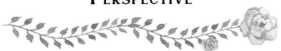

We are guests on this earth. We must all live and die. All of us. No one is immortal! This pandemic is unfortunate, and as my dad would say, my mouth is sharp or is running because I am safe, healthy, and still have a job. But let's look at the other side of this. It has given us time to reflect. We are inside looking out.

There is a superior force at work. Humanity was forced to pause, take a deep breath, and press the reset button.

The earth is an entrustment. We must treat it as such. While in this pandemic look for opportunities to help and defrost your heart. Most of all, don't operate as you always have.

Take what you will from this pandemic but take something!

Discussion & Reflection Questions:

- Have you become numb?
- Have you "safely" gone out of your way to help someone during this pandemic?
- What has changed for you with all that is going on?

Use the following journal pages to write out your thoughts.

SEPTEMBER 11, 2020

We just never know. Hence, we must be intentional about every moment of our lives.

Life is a gift from The Almighty Father, and we are not called to slumber. We must shed all laziness and fear and LIVE our purpose!

I know, I'm being serious, and I think I deserve the right to be. I have shared my life with you, so I think of you as family. So, I am preaching today.

Do you think the financial analysts, firefighters, paramedics, office assistants, policemen, mothers, fathers, daughters, and sons thought they would not make it home on September 11th, 2001? They did not! They had plans, they procrastinated like us, they made promises, they had dreams, they wanted second chances, they wanted to say I'm sorry, they wanted to write a book, they wanted to stop doing something or the other. They wanted to do better like we all do, but wanting is not enough. There is no time! We must do!

I find it ironic that I am writing the last chapter of my book on this day. It is shouting at me! This day in 2020! Look at where we are. We are in the middle of a pandemic, and we barely know what comes next.

My point is that we must live!

I have decided not to be a hypocrite and pine for a failed marriage. I have decided to live like I am telling you to do. We cannot reach the end of our lives and look back only to realize we lived it in another man's image. What? That is not okay!

We cannot blame others for choices we did not make and for courage we did not have. I shared my story with you to give you hope, courage, and many thoughts to ponder about your life.

I am doing well today. I am happy with my choices. I am placing less blame on my ex for choices I did not make. I am forgiving myself for being naive and trusting, but I am not saying I will not trust again or that I will not still be naïve. I will just be intentional and careful. There is no rush.

There is no rush to marry someone when you hardly know yourself. There is no rush to have children when you are a child yourself. There is no rush to acquire material things when you have debt (talking to myself here, not you). There is no rush to remove the speck in another's eye when you have a log in yours. There is no rush to resent others when you should look within. There is no rush to answer or be right. There is no rush to get wherever it is that takes you away from your family. There is no rush to get to that other man or woman who is not your spouse or partner. There is no rush to give time to the undeserving. There is no rush to go away from God.

There just is no rush. Let's stop as the pandemic has asked and take stock! Please!

However, there is no time for petty jealousy, there is no time to be a second class citizen, there is no time for blame, there is no time for self-pity, there is no time for laziness, there is no time for taking advantage of others or situations, there is no time for cheating, lying, stealing, there is no time for playing victim, there is no time for excuses, there is no time to come back and say I love you or I'm sorry, there is no time for hiding, there is no time to wait for the next chance, there is no time to heal from the last beating, there is no time to see if they will change, there is no time to file that report, there is no time to pack your things, there is no time to stand and stare.

Move!

There is just no time.

I don't think the people who lost their lives on September 11th, 2001 and those who are losing their lives today for so many reasons, thought they wouldn't have time.

I am healing and learning to stop blaming people for my situation but taking it in my stride and looking at my story as a gift that I get to share with you.

I am grateful for life, breath, purpose, second chances, and time. Thank you, Father.

This is how I am doing after the fog lifted and I gained clarity from chaos and confusion!

God bless you on your journey. Godspeed!

Epilogue

I have sent the final draft to my editor, and I'm lying down, feeling like, *Oh shoot! It's gone. You better have said all you want to say.* But then I'm like, *Nah, there'll be another book.*

I keep remembering stuff I want to share. So, I'm going to include one last chapter. One last chapter to tell you that it wasn't always so bad.

Yes, there were good times. I mean, c'mon, we had three children together. I know you're all wondering why I stayed for almost seventeen years if I wasn't happy. I was happy. I did go in with every intention to grow old with my man. I was in love, and I believe he was in love, too. Being in love was just not enough for us. I question everything now. I think back on all the good times, and I question it all. Was it in my head? Was I creating what I wanted? Was I forcing it? No, I wasn't. Right?

We met coincidentally at the mall, and he had all the arrogance and dark, tall handsomeness I never knew I craved. He approached me with authority and had an accent. A Nigerian accent? No way! How was it possible? He asked for my number, and I played hard to get and asked for his, told him I would call him.

I was smitten. He was determined. Have you ever heard guys say, "I knew I was going to marry you the first time I saw you"? And then there's "I knew I loved you the first time I saw you." Yes, I got the marry comment. Sorry to burst your bubble. It's not possible to love someone the moment you meet them. You may feel an attraction, even a connection, but none of you can tell me it's love. Nope! Not buying it!

When he told me he knew he would marry me when he met me, I felt like I was the luckiest girl in the world. I was walking on clouds. He would call and we would talk on the phone for hours. We went out on a few dates and started to do everything together.

He would always ask me if I was okay, and I complained that it made me uncomfortable and then later on I wanted him to ask me, and he didn't. I met his friends and talked to his family on the phone, and he talked to my mom a few times (my dad was still playing hard ball—I should have let him). We had a few incidents that just seemed like growing pains to me. No big deal.

Our chemistry was better than I had experienced in other relationships, so that was another plus. He didn't worship the ground I walked on, but I was blind and didn't really think I needed that. Ladies, you must marry a guy that worships the ground you walk on, literally. I don't care what anyone says. He needs to give you all he has. I am not talking about riches, I am talking about generosity, sharing, and ownership. I was okay with what he offered because I really didn't have much to compare it to since I wasn't a serial dater. I must have had an inkling that he wasn't all that because I embellished with my parents and big sister's friends that would ask all the prying questions.

We made plans. We had dreams. And I worked hard to make those dreams come true. He may argue that he worked hard too, in the beginning, but I am still confused about what happened there. I know we made plans, but I feel like there was our plan and the plan. I often pray I am wrong, but I'll never know.

We had our son, and it was heavenly. He was as hands-on as I could dream of with our son, and our love blossomed. If anyone told me I would be writing this today instead of having dinner with my complete family (husband included), I might have fought them. We had our second daughter, and I thought he became less involved because we had a nanny and she was a girl, but by the time my last one came, he wasn't the same as he was with the first. Please don't say everyone is different with their first because I know! Time went on, and I was not the mother I thought I would be, and I did not have the husband I thought I would have. I fell out of love from too many disappointments and broken promises.

Yes, we were in love. We had our song. We spent all our time together, and I love him. Yes, I say love. I didn't stutter. I am no longer in love with him, but I love him. I don't wish him harm, but I will never be a fool for him or any human again. Talking about being a fool, I need to work on that because people just see me (all 5'11 inches of me) and think they can take me for a fool. They sometimes succeed. Yeah, there's healing work to be done.

I lie here and my heart aches. I don't want to be alone. I don't want to be divorced. I don't want to give someone else my heart. I want my husband, the one I spent so many years building with, but he's not here. I divorced him, and my heart aches for him today. Why does it hurt so much? Why do I have to be logical? Why couldn't he just hold my aching heart?

Perspective

Yes, people, I am human. And we are family, so I will tell you the truth. It's not easy. I get lonely, but I am lonely for the wrong thing. You deserve to long for and wait for true love. I hear it's really nice. I hear you actually don't have to play games. I hear you can trust the other person.

Be strong and keep yourself for the right one. Don't be scared to be single forever. There's someone out there made just for you.

It is totally worth it! I know, and that's why I am fighting for it! I am scared that I might end up an old maid, but it is the love I hear in songs, read in books, and see in old couples that keeps me longing....

I think I'm finally done. I am finally crying. Wailing, actually. I lost! This time.

Not sure where this chapter will be in my book, but it's my last!

Thank you to my love for a taste of what could have been. I know I am worthy of so much more, and I will never again settle for less.

I am stronger today than I have ever been.

I am free.

RESOURCES

Books that helped me

- **Boundaries: When to Say YES, When to Say NO, to Take Control of Your Life**
  by John Townsend and Henry Cloud
- **The Path Made Clear : Discovering Your Life's Direction and Purpose**
  by Oprah Winfrey
- **Disarming the Narcissist: Surviving and Thriving with the Self-Absorbed**
  by Wendy T. Behary MSW LCSW (Author), Daniel J. Siegel MD (Preface), Jeffrey Young PhD (Foreword)
- **Permanent Happiness: The only way to find peace, joy, and your life-given purpose**
  by Iyabo Y Ojikutu MD
- **Reflections Of A Man** ***1st Edition***
  by Mr. Amari Soul (Author)
- **He's Lying Sis: Uncover the Truth Behind His Words and Actions** ***Volume 1 Paperback – February 26, 2019***
  by Stephan Labossiere (Author), C. Nzingha Smith (Editor), Stephan Speaks (Contributor)
- **The Man God Has For You: 7 Traits to Help You Determine Your Life Partner** ***Paperback – July 28, 2017***
  by Stephan Labossiere (Author), Stephan Speaks (Author)
- **Finding Love After Heartbreak: Volume I** ***Paperback – April 8, 2019***
  by Stephan Labossiere (Author), Stephan Speaks (Author)
- **Her Paperback** ***February 11, 2017***
  by Pierre Alex Jeanty (Author), Carla Dupont (Editor), Sarah Plamondon (Editor)

* <u>**Ashes of Her Love**</u> ***Paperback – August 12, 2019***
  by Pierre Alex Jeanty (Author), Jada Hawkins (Author), Carla DuPont (Editor)

* <u>**Have a New Kid by Friday: How To Change Your Child's Attitude, Behavior & Character In 5 Days**</u>
  by Kevin Leman

Daily practices that helped me

* **I get my strength from God first and foremost**
* **Prayer**
* **My support system**
* **Music: all kinds, from R&B to Gospel, to Pop, to Classical, to Country, to Afro beats. Music does soothe the soul.**
* **Meditation: Calm App**
* **Relaxing walks in nature**
* **A good cry or laugh**
* **Exercise**
* **Work: financial independence and purpose**
* **My children: they need me**
* **Therapy: mental wellness**
* **Physical wellness: self-care**
* **And of course, WRITING!**

GLOSSARY

FLYING MONKEY

The term "flying monkeys" is another way of saying "abuse by proxy" or having someone else do the bidding of, in this case, a narcissist. The term flying monkey was coined after the flying monkeys in the Wizard of Oz that were under the spell of the Wicked Witch of the East, to do her bidding against Dorothy and her friends.

This common narcissistic tactic uses friends and family of the victim to spy on them, spread gossip while painting the narcissist as the victim and their target as the perpetrator. Flying monkeys can be your friends, family, co-workers, or the narcissist's friends, family, or co-workers before you got there. To maintain the illusion of the power they have over you, the narcissist will employ the use of third parties, through which they will attempt to continue control and manipulate you.

Source: https://narcissistabusesupport.com/red-flags/use-flying-monkeys/

GASLIGHTING

Gaslighting is a form of psychological manipulation in which a person or a group covertly sows seeds of doubt in a targeted individual or group, making them question their own memory, perception, or judgment, often evoking in them cognitive dissonance and other changes, including low self-esteem. Using denial, misdirection, contradiction, and misinformation, gaslighting involves attempts to destabilize the victim and delegitimize the victim's beliefs. Instances can range from the denial by an abuser that previous abusive incidents occurred, to belittling the victim's emotions and feelings, to the staging of bizarre events by the abuser with the intention of disorienting the victim.

Source: https://en.wikipedia.org/wiki/Gaslighting

STONEWALLING

Stonewalling is when one partner disengages from the other and becomes unavailable—like a stone wall has been put between the them.

A person can stonewall by physically leaving the scene or just sitting silently without responding. Either way, it's avoiding conversations or solving problems by being uncooperative or by shutting down for days or weeks. Stonewalling also includes dismissing everything the other person says as boring, unreasonable, or unimportant as a reason to not participate.

Source: https://www.ananiasfoundation.org/stonewalling/?gclid=Cj0KCQjwk8b7BRCaARIsAARRTL5ORyW-AG-zZPQn0gV3w067TIziKOa-xlkSxKElgCaR06fqElTwuMpUaA-h2uEALw_wcB

✻ EMPATH

Not every sensitive person is an empath. The definition of empathy is the ability to understand someone's thoughts and feelings from their perspective instead of your own.

So, the first thing you'll notice about empaths is that they can understand you even if they haven't any experiences that are similar to yours. Conversations with them flow effortlessly, and they form close relationships with ease.

There are a few core values many empaths share: meaningful relationships, non-judgment, and deep concern for the well-being of others.

Large groups of people can be quite overwhelming for an empath, as they absorb the emotions and energy around them. They also value their alone time, as they can benefit from taking a step back from other people's lives.

Source: https://blog.mindvalley.com/empath-definition/

✻ NARCISSIST

Narcissistic personality disorder—one of several types of personality disorders—is a mental condition in which people have an inflated sense of their own importance, a deep need for excessive attention and admiration, troubled relationships, and a lack of empathy for others. But behind this mask of extreme confidence lies a fragile self-esteem that's vulnerable to the slightest criticism.

Source: https://www.mayoclinic.org/diseases-conditions/narcissistic-personality-disorder/symptoms-causes/syc-20366662#:~:text=Narcissistic%20personality%20disorder%20%E2%80%94%20one%20of,lack%20of%20empathy%20for%20others

✻ BOAZ

Boaz was the husband of Ruth, as documented in the book of Ruth in the Bible. He represents one of the good men that are worth waiting for.

✻ LOVE BOMBING

Love bombing is the practice of showering a person with excessive affection and attention in order to gain control or significantly influence their behavior. The love bomber's attention might feel good, but the motive is all about manipulation. What separates love bombing from just regular honeymoon feelings is an abrupt switch—one moment they may be totally idealizing their partner, and the next, they'll cut them down to size in an effort to control them.

✻ EMOTIONAL MANIPULATION

Emotional manipulators often use mind games to seize power in a relationship. The ultimate goal is to use that power to control the other person. A healthy relationship is based on trust, understanding, and mutual respect. This is true of personal relationships, as well as professional ones. Sometimes, people seek to exploit these elements of a relationship in order to benefit themselves in some way. The signs of emotional manipulation can be subtle. They're often hard to identify, especially when they're happening to you.

Source: https://www.healthline.com/health/mental-health/emotional-manipulation

✻ EMOTIONAL ABUSE

If you feel scared or confused around your partner, or doubt yourself when you're talking with them, you may be experiencing emotional abuse. An emotional abuser's goal is to undermine another person's feelings of self-worth and independence. In an emotionally abusive relationship, you may feel that there is no way out or that without your partner you'll have nothing. Emotional abuse is a form of domestic and family violence.

Source: https://au.reachout.com/articles/what-is-emotional-abuse

- **PARACONFUSHOCKED**

  A state of paranoia, confusion, and shock.

- **VIOCONFUNAKED**

  A feeling of being violated, confused, and naked at the same time.

- **BABA MO DUPE**

  Father Lord I give thanks (translated to English from Yoruba, a Nigerian dialect spoken in the southwestern parts of Nigeria).

Acknowledgments

- ***Thank you, Lord***, for unconditional love that only you can give, for your mercy on my life, for the strength to get up and walk, for provision, for the honor of a relationship with you, the grace to hear from you, and for the helpers you send me in all forms to walk with me, stand by me, and guide me through this earth life. Father, I don't take it for granted. I am in so much awe to be your child. Baba mo dupe!*

- ***My friends and family***, I am purposely not going to call names because you are just too many. I still don't understand how I got so lucky for all the chats, the conversations, the loving comfort, the pep talks, the laughter, the tears, the unasked questions, the unwavering support. I am so grateful and appreciate each and every one of you for your special and unique contribution to my journey and healing.

- ***Meredith Dunn***, my book whisperer. Thank you! Thank you for pulling these words out of me. I know it was hard sometimes, but we did it. Thank you for respecting my story and wishes. Thank you for joining my family. More books to come!

- ***My creative team***, you are so many. All the ideas that came to life! Wow! I just told you what I needed, and you made it happen. I wish you prosperity in all your different trades. You are truly gifted.

- ***My readers!*** You pushed me to write and show up. You made me not feel sorry for myself because I knew you were on the other side of this book. You gave me courage I didn't know I had, helped me find words I didn't know I could write, and helped me transcribe my pain and joy to life.

Thank you all!

**See Glossary on page 270 for definition.*